CROSS-CULTURAL ESSENTIALS 7

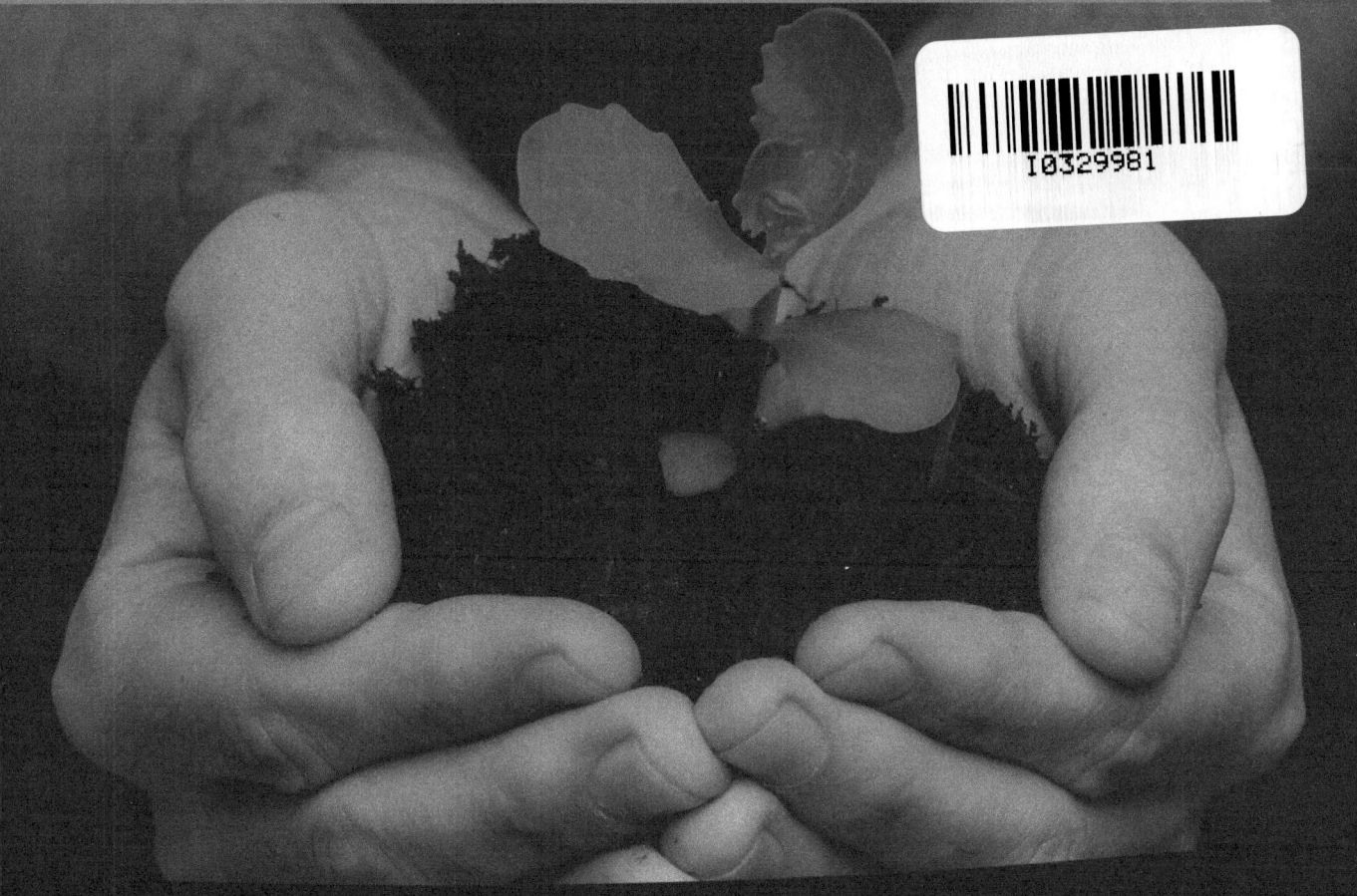

WORD, IDENTITY, LIFE, DISCIPLESHIP

A FRAMEWORK FOR UNDERSTANDING HOW TRUTH IMPACTS PEOPLE AND CHURCHES

W.I.L.D: Word, Identity, Life, Discipleship
Understanding life, growth and fruit within discipleship and church planting

Church Foundations, Module 7 of the Cross-Cultural Essentials Curriculum

Copyright © 2019, 2015 AccessTruth

Version 1.2

ISBN: 978-0-9944270-0-7

All Rights Reserved. Except as may be permitted by the Copyright Act, no part of this publication may be reproduced in any form or by any means without prior permission from the publisher. Requests for permission should be made to info@accesstruth.com

Unless otherwise indicated, all Scripture quotations are taken from the Holy Bible, New Living Translation, copyright © 1996, 2004. Used by permission of Tyndale House Publishers, Inc., Wheaton, Illinois 60189. All rights reserved.

Published by AccessTruth
PO Box 8087
Baulkham Hills NSW 2153
Australia

Email: info@accesstruth.com
Web: accesstruth.com

Cover and interior design by Matthew Hillier
Edited by Simon Glover

Table of Contents

About the Cross-Cultural Essentials Curriculum 5

TUTORIAL 7.1 7
God is building His Church

TUTORIAL 7.2 13
Building, Body, Bride

TUTORIAL 7.3 19
Coworkers with God

TUTORIAL 7.4 25
Clarity in church building work

TUTORIAL 7.5 33
Word. Identity. Life. Discipleship.

TUTORIAL 7.6 41
Access to the Bible

TUTORIAL 7.7 47
Engaging at a worldview level

TUTORIAL 7.8 55
The authority of God's Word

TUTORIAL 7.9 63
The complete Narrative

TUTORIAL 7.10 71
Making use of God's Word

TUTORIAL 7.11 79
Understanding true identity

TUTORIAL 7.12 87
The Narrative of the Church

TUTORIAL 7.13 95
One Body in Christ

TUTORIAL 7.14 103
Viewing others according to truth

TUTORIAL 7.15 111
Introduction to 'Life'

TUTORIAL 7.16 119
A relationship with Jesus

TUTORIAL 7.17 127
The purpose for which we exist

TUTORIAL 7.18 137
Form, function, fulfilment

TUTORIAL 7.19 149
Introduction to 'Discipleship'

TUTORIAL 7.20 157
Disciples of the Master

TUTORIAL 7.21 165
Applying Truth in the walk of faith

TUTORIAL 7.22 177
Equipped for service

About the Cross-Cultural Essentials Curriculum

It's no secret that there are still millions of people in the world living in "unreached" or "least-reached" areas. If you look at the maps, the stats, and the lists of people group names, it's almost overwhelming. The people represented by those numbers can't find out about God, or who Jesus Christ is, or what He did for them because there's no Bible in their language or church in their area – they have *no access* to Truth.

So you could pack a suitcase and jump on a plane, but then what? How would you spend your first day? How would you start learning language? When would you tell them about Jesus? Where would you start? The truth is that a mature, grounded fellowship of God's children doesn't just "happen" in an unreached area or even in your neighborhood. When we speak the Truth, we need to have the confidence that it is still the same Truth when it gets through our hearer's language, culture and worldview grid.

The *Cross-Cultural Essentials* curriculum, made up of 10 individual modules, forms a comprehensive training course. Its main goal is to help equip believers to be effective in providing people access to God's Truth through evangelism and discipleship. The *Cross-Cultural Essentials* curriculum makes it easy to be better equipped for teaching the whole narrative of the Bible, for learning about culture and worldview and for planting a church and seeing it grow.

More information on the curriculum can be found at *accesstruth.com*

Introduction to Module 7

Module 7 answers the question, Do we need a goal when we are involved in church planting and discipleship? Then, using an outline that has been developed by experienced church planters in a number of contexts, it describes four different areas of growth in the Body - Word, Identity, Life and Discipleship - and how to encourage growth in each area. Practical help and examples are given to equip participants with principles, and an understanding of the realities of each of these areas of growth in a real context.

ABOUT THE CROSS-CULTURAL ESSENTIALS CURRICULUM

How to use this module

Read / watch / listen: Read through the tutorial. If you have an online account at *accesstruth.com*, or the DVD associated with this module you can watch the video or listen to the audio of the tutorial.

Discussion Points: At the end of each tutorial there are discussion points. It may be helpful to write down your answers so you can better process your thoughts. If you are doing the tutorials in a group, use these points to guide the discussion.

Activities: Some tutorials have activities that can involve practical, real-life tasks or may just ask for a written answer.

7.1 God is building His Church

 OBJECTIVES OF THIS TUTORIAL

This tutorial introduces Module 7 and some of the key foundations for the Church; what the Church is, and how God, the Author, is working to build His Church.

God as Author

If you have already completed other parts of the *Cross-Cultural Essentials* curriculum (and we hope you have at very least been through Modules 1 and 2) you will know that we are very consciously trying to present a cohesive picture of God as Author. Hopefully that has come out clearly as we've followed His Narrative and seen Him at work in Creation and as He's interacted with that Creation, especially with His image-bearing race. Implicit in the metaphor of God as Author is the concept that He does not act randomly or arbitrarily. And even though He is *responsive* this does not mean that He is *reactive*, in the sense of being dictated to by circumstances or by the actions of others. He is the Initiator, and what He initiates or creates, is according to His plan and perfectly aligned with His being, His character.

In this Module (7), we want to introduce a picture of the Church - and churches - that fits very clearly with this view of God as Author. We believe, and want to clearly demonstrate, that He has carefully planned His Church in a way that is consistent with who He is and the way He has always functioned. He has specific intentions for each local church that are intended to play a unique and indispensable part in His overall Plan. He puts within those local churches, people with the gifts and abilities to do what He wants that church to do - within its local context and beyond.

What we mean by "church"

Before we go any further, we should probably take a moment to define this term we are going to be using a lot in these tutorials - Church and church. Our western history has embedded a number of meanings into the word "church" that are not necessarily helpful. English dictionaries commonly include these definitions:

(1) **A building for public worship** - "They renovated the church"

(2) **The clergy or officialdom of a religious body** - "The church laid out its doctrine"

(3) **A body or organization of religious believers** - "It's on the church website"

(4) **Public worship** - "They attend church on Sundays"

(5) **The clerical profession** - "He went into the church as a career"

In these resources, when we talk about "the Church" (big "C") we are referring to all those who've trusted Jesus as their Saviour in the period between the day of Pentecost and the future day when we are reunited forever with Him. This is the group or body that the New Testament writers usually called the ecclesia (sometimes spelled ekklesia), a term borrowed from Greek culture for a gathering or assembly of people who'd been called out from their normal activities for a specific purpose. And when we speak of a church (small "c") we are referring, or course, to a specific group or body that is a part of the universal Church or Ecclesia - still a "gathering or assembly of called out people", but in a specific place and a particular time. So by church, we are not referring to a building, or a group of officials, or something that someone goes to or does on a particular day.

Hopefully this amazing thing that we're struggling to describe here in words, or propositional terms, will continue to emerge much more clearly as we look at it in *Narrative* terms - in the way God has actually brought it into being, given it life, interacted with it, equipped it, expressed His love toward it, and given it purpose. Because when we spend too much time defining the Church in bulleted points it tends to "flatten it" and make it seem like something cold and theoretical. So even though we will sometimes define things about the Church and its purpose conceptually, we don't want to ever lose sight of the reality that for God the Author, this whole subject is very real and personal and even, can we say, *emotional*...but more about that soon.

What time is it?

So, God the Author has carefully laid out the plot for His real life Narrative of how history will play out...and He's arranged it so that most of this last period we're in now is the *time of the Church*. There are, of course, other ways of describing this period since Pentecost... it is the *time of grace* and the time of the *New Testament* (or Covenant). But the thing that God is doing right now is completing His Church.

Temple building

One of God the Author's favorite metaphors that He uses in His Narrative to describe His Church is that of a *building*. More specifically, it is a temple that is being built. This of course ties into the enormously important Narrative threads from the Old Covenant with its Tabernacle, and later Temple, in Jerusalem. When Jesus came to the earth and died and rose again, the Old Covenant with its priesthood, sacrifices and Temple, was fulfilled and superseded... something the book of Hebrews makes clear. Now the Spirit of God is living in His people.

In the first of Paul's letters to the believers in the southern Greek city of Corinth, he challenges the ecclesia to live in light of the reality that they are *God's temple* (1 Corinthians 3:10-17). A few years later he extends the image when he writes to the believers in Ephesus, famous for its temple to the goddess Artemis (Ephesians 2:20-22). He says that all believers are God's house, a holy temple for the Lord and a dwelling place where God lives by His Spirit. This building is structurally bound together by Jesus Himself, and is being built on the Truth-foundations about Him that He revealed to us through His designated storytellers - His apostles and prophets. Picturing stone masons carefully choosing, shaping and then placing individual blocks into a public building, Paul says that we are each being added into God's temple like that.

A mystery revealed

So this careful building process is what God is fully committed to in this time of history and He's doing it - of course - in a way that is perfectly consistent with who He is. All the things about Him that He shows us through His written Narrative are also playing out in this time through the building of the Church. When you stop and think about that, it's absolutely astounding. In fact, Paul, the former Pharisee who was recruited so dramatically by Jesus Himself for His Cause, calls it a mystery...a mysterious plan.

It is not a mystery in the sense of something unknowable - God did reveal this plan to Paul and the other apostles as he said in his letter to the believers in Ephesus (Ephesians 3:3-10) and in the capital of the Empire, Rome (Romans 16:25). It's also because it is something that is in the process of being demonstrated more fully each day - each time God's Truth penetrates a human heart or a new community; when someone listens to His Narrative and believes it instead of their own story; when they respond in faith and His Spirit joins them to the Ecclesia; when a scattered group of believers in a town begins to come together to worship Him; when His Word is translated into a language that speaks right to the heart of His people; when His children submit to the authority of His Word; when a worldview assumption is realigned to His absolute Truth; when someone takes on the task of discipling a younger believer; when His children are willing to sacrifice and even suffer to share the Good News with someone or to make it available in a new area - this is the Mystery of the Church being revealed, the Narrative of who God *IS* being written in the hearts and lives and gatherings of His children.

Reflecting His glory

And why is He doing this? Why does He choose this means for writing the latest installments of His Great Narrative? Paul gives us the answer in what he wrote to the Ephesians. He is using the Church to display His wisdom in its rich variety. As God's Spirit gives life and all the necessary resources for His Church to survive and grow, God's glory is reflected and made known to everyone who sees this happening, both now and also outside the bounds of this physical world. When God's purposes are achieved through His image-bearers who were corrupted by sin, but now are new creations because of Christ, that demonstrates just how amazing He is. And when His people unite their hearts in praise, their wills to please Him, and their efforts to achieve His purposes…then it becomes an amazing picture that even the most powerful spirit beings can only wonder at.

An invitation to be involved

But this is not something that God achieves by just doing it to the Church. Amazingly, He chooses to involve us - His Church, His churches, and His people - in the process itself of the building of His Temple. Again, this fits with a thread we've traced through the Narrative - an extension of who He is. He chooses to involve, even to work as partners or co-workers with, people who will humbly follow His lead. He never abdicates responsibility - "Oh, you just do it how you see fit". Through the Narrative; with Adam and Eve, Abraham, Moses, the craftsmen building the Tabernacle and Temple, the kings of Israel, even with the Lord Jesus Himself…God has always been directly involved, clearly stating how things should be done so they line up with who He is, then giving the patience, strength, wisdom, etc., to get the job done. And it is a genuine collaboration. He wants His human co-workers to use their minds, their time, money, energy and wills… to really give themselves as wholeheartedly to the Task as He does.

So God is indeed building His Church, but He invites us to be vitally involved in the building project. And because, as we've noted, He's following a design that in every way reflects who He is, we have a responsibility to, (1) understand that design, and (2) work accordingly. This is something that hasn't always been sufficiently appreciated in the Church, even by those who are committed to being involved in sharing the Gospel with others. The Lord's apostle, Paul, was one who obviously did have a real vision for this *clarity* and *care* that should characterize our participation in God's building of His Church.

Careful master builders

As we followed the Acts Narrative, we saw this come out in the way Paul approached his role of planting and strengthening churches in places like Antioch, Thessalonica, Ephesus and Corinth. In the letters Paul writes to individuals and local fellowships, it becomes even more obvious that he is working according to a "blueprint" that God's Spirit was showing him. And he uses this imagery specifically with the church in Corinth, describing them as God's building project that he, as an expert carpenter, began right at the foundations (1 Corinthians 3:9-10). Anyone else contributing further to this project, he warns, needs to be careful that their work lines up with the foundation, that is Jesus Christ Himself.

Following the threads

The intention of this Module (7) is to bundle together key Narrative threads that run all the way through God's Word and label them in ways that help us to understand more about how God works. As we'll see in the next Tutorial, this is not so that we can pretend we totally understand all there is to know about the wonderful mystery that is His Church. Nor do we want to reduce to theoretical formulas something so precious to Him as His *Body*, His *Bride*. But to really contribute something of lasting value to His Building means investing our whole being, like God does. It involves our wills and emotions, but it also requires that we engage our intellects and our minds, and ask Him to give us real clarity and insights so that we can be adequately equipped as His building co-workers.

? DISCUSSION POINTS

1. What do you think of the idea that God is building His Church according to a careful plan? As you look at what you know of the Church and churches, does that appear to be the reality? If you do see a gap between the idea of God's careful planning on the one hand, and then the reality on the other, reflect on why that may be.

2. As you've thought about serving the Lord, how much has the idea of working with Him and others to build His Church featured in those thoughts? Do you tend to see your service for Him that way, or is that a relatively new concept for you? Please share any observations you have.

7.2 Building, Body, Bride

✓ OBJECTIVES OF THIS TUTORIAL

This tutorial reminds us that God is personally invested in relating to us - as individuals and as groups - and that the primary relationship He is pursuing on the earth right now is with the Church, His Body. He invites us to contribute in the construction of His Building, the nourishment and growth of His Body and the preparation of His Bride.

Last Time
We considered how God the Author has carefully laid out the plot of His Great Narrative in ways that are consistent with who He is. At this time in that unfolding Narrative, He is focused on His Church - the gathering of His called-out people that He loves dearly. He is carefully building a Temple for Himself, precisely placing each "stone": people who have trusted in Jesus for salvation. This was previously a mystery but it was revealed to the apostles and it continues to be unveiled day by day as He extends this project. He invites us, His people, to be involved in that building work, but we have to understand and work in ways that are consistent with who He is... according to the plan that we find embedded in His Word.

Personally invested
Something that we've seen emerge from God's Narrative over and over again is just how personally He is invested in His Creation, particularly in the relationship He is seeking with His image-bearing race. The whole point of creation was to have an environment, which would speak to its human inhabitants of His love, faithfulness, wisdom and power...an environment that would serve the purposes of mutual dialogue He clearly delights in. Even after the human race rejected this relationship, He remained committed, providing a way for them to relate that would not violate His perfectly righteous character. We see this deep personal investment too in the individual relationships that He nurtured - with Abraham, Moses, David, and then most amazingly, in the relationship of God the Father and Spirit with Jesus Christ, the Son.

But we also see that God relates to people, not only as individuals, but as groups… the human race, Adam's descendants, the inhabitants of the earth, the Egyptians, the tribes in Palestine, and of course, the nation of Israel. This last was a tempestuous and often tragic relationship as God's Chosen People time and time again turned away from Him. But He constantly testified to His unchanging love for them. They were *His*, He said; His *special treasure* set apart through the Covenant He made with them among the rocks and sand of Sinai, after rescuing them from Egypt (Exodus 19:4).

Over the centuries God often used the most personal, intimate terms in speaking to His People. In the words of His prophet Jeremiah (Jeremiah 3:19-20) He said to them that He would love to treat them as His children, and had looked forward to them calling Him Father. Tragically though, the relationship has broken His heart…He feels more like a loving husband whose unfaithful wife has left Him. But despite all their lack of gratitude and trust, their faithlessness and regular rejection, God was willing to live among His people, the nation of Israel… to have a special presence right in their community.

A new kind of relationship

And then the New Covenant was initiated through the death of Jesus and a new era began in God's engagement with His Creation. He continues to love the world of course and to seek out any who'll respond from His lost race of image-bearers. And He has not given up on His chosen nation, Israel, but the relationship had always been underpinned by the Promise of the Messiah He would send.

Of course they failed to recognise, and violently rejected Him, when He came to live among them as a man. So a new Covenant, defining a new kind of relationship, was drawn up. On the day of Pentecost, God's Spirit came into the world in order to live with those people who by faith have been fully identified with God's beloved Son, Jesus. But, as has always been the case, God relates to them, and to us, not only as individuals but also as a Group…gathered together in Christ, joined together by the Spirit. During the time in history we live in now, His greatest expression of delight and affection is reserved for the Church, His special, blood-bought people.

The Body

In the last tutorial (7.1), we focused on the picture embedded in the Narrative, of God building a Temple. But as we said, this is not just a detached, impersonal exercise, with Him as a distant Architect. Far from it! This is very personal, very real, and very immediate for God. To help us understand this in more than just theoretical propositions, He has used two other images or metaphors that help us feel it in an intuitive and emotional way. In fact, it's worth pondering whether as the great, wise Author, God threaded these things into creation and human experience, in part at least, so we would have these images to help us understand His relationship with His Ecclesia. The first of these is the *Body*; certainly in His Narrative He doesn't only liken the Church to a body, His Body, but He says it actually *is* that. He says that Christ is the Head, and we are His legs, arms, feet, etc.

Unity in the Body

Sitting in his rented house in Rome, while waiting for his trial before the Emperor, Paul was reflecting on the topic of *authority* in a letter to his friends in Ephesus (Ephesians 1:22). He reminded them that Jesus Christ is in a place of honor and power with God, and that He has the ultimate and final authority in everything, both in the present and future. God has given Him this authority for our sake, the Church...because He is our head, and we are His Body. A little further on in the letter (Ephesians 2:14-15), Paul adds the amazing thought for the ethnically mixed group of believers, that because we've all been identified with the death of Jesus' *physical* body at Golgotha, any superficial distinctions such as race no longer exist for us as His *spiritual* Body, the Church.

As with anything or anyone we care deeply about, Jesus has hopes and dreams for this Group that is so much a part of Him...this Body that shares His identity. But with God, it's never just a dream of what *could* be; it's also a declaration of what *will* be. To ensure that it does happen, Jesus has provided all the raw materials - the Truth - and He continues to give His Body every possible assistance in utilizing those resources. As His mouthpiece, guided by His Spirit, Paul articulates the Vision and Purpose that Jesus, the Head, has for His Body (Ephesians 4:13-16). He wants it to become mature and in every way to reflect Him so there are no anomalies between the Head and Body. He is looking for perfect unity within His Body, a healthy, loving and growing Group of His People.

The Bride

Paul, still trying to help the Ephesians understand just how personally invested Jesus is in His Church, blends the imagery of a Body with that of a *Bride*. This, of course, ties right back to the very beginning, when God knew that the first human being He had made, Adam, needed a companion who was of the same race. Seeing her for the first time, Adam immediately knew that this person was designed exactly to share his life with him. They fulfilled each other in a way that no other could. God's Narrative observes that two humans bonded in marriage in this way now become *one* in a very real sense, their identities are merged inseparably. Paul says that this is exactly the case of the bond of Jesus Christ and His Body, His Church.

Bought at immeasurable cost

But again, this is not just a disembodied reality that can be somehow studied in a laboratory, or reduced to formulas, or even, ultimately, to be pinned down as doctrine. Just as the Church itself is a mystery in the process of being revealed, so too is the husband-like care and love that Christ feels toward His Church. It's an unfolding mystery because there is no limit to it. After all, He gave up everything for the Church. Like a husband who is willing to forgo His own rights, including the basic right of survival and self-preservation - He was willing to die for the Church. Looking ahead and seeing the desperately lost people who put their trust in Him, His heart went out to them. He was determined to make that group of people His own; to set it apart as His special companion; to meld its identity with His own; to unlock the potential He could see in these individuals working together as one Body for His majestic and wonderful purposes.

Marriage in the First Century

This picture of the Church as Bride is particularly rich in imagery when viewed through the lens of the culture in which the New Testament Narrative was recorded. In the first century, people from a Judean cultural background would have understood marriage rather differently from the way we do. The first step was the betrothal, a legally binding contract drawn up between the groom and father of the bride. According to their traditions, at that point, the marriage had already taken place, even though the couple did not live together as man and wife until later - sometimes years later - when all the financial obligations in the contract were dealt with. As we'll remember from the events surrounding Jesus' birth, this was the situation of Mary and Joseph when she became pregnant with Jesus. We can imagine the groom longing for the day when he could finally go in procession with his friends and shout out to let the bride's family and friends know that he was coming to claim her. Then, the third and final stage was the wedding feast, when everyone was invited to publicly celebrate the marriage at the groom's home.

When Paul was writing the second of his letters to the church in Corinth - a city famous for immoral cultish practices - he urged them not to waver in their devotion to the Lord Jesus (2 Corinthians 11:2). He yearns for them to be like a pure, betrothed young woman waiting for her groom to claim her. Jesus' much-loved disciple John was also given insights, through the rich imagery of marriage, of how the Lord feels about His Church. In the Revelation that John received from God of future events, he heard people around God's throne rejoicing because the time had come for the wedding feast of the Lamb, the One who'd given His life in her place. She was ready for Him, they said, perfectly clothed in the good things God had led His people to do for Him (Revelation 19:7-8). Then a little later, John records that he sees the Church coming to meet the Lord, just "like a bride, beautifully dressed for her husband."

Architect and Building

In the previous tutorial we noted the metaphor of a *Building*, particularly God building a place for Himself to live, that emerges at different points of the Narrative. Under the New Covenant the Great *Architect* and builder is carefully building His Church. He invites us to be part of this construction project. And so we need His help in understanding the blueprint of what He intends to accomplish, and insights into how He is going about it so that we can be wise master builders.

Head and Body

But the Church is not something He's creating 'out there', a pet project He picks up now and then. It's actually a part of who He is. Jesus Christ is the *Head* and the Church is His *Body* - His arms and legs, hands and feet, living and doing His work in the created world. He has given life to this Body and now He is nourishing and encouraging it to grow towards a healthy maturity so it can do, and be, all He intends. We have a responsibility to understand what that health and maturity looks like so we can work alongside Him to encourage the existing Body and cultivate its outward growth.

Groom and Bride

This is not something He's doing out of obligation or necessity, just because He is attached to the Church...far from it. The image of a Bride helps us feel what Jesus, the Groom, feels towards His Church, the eager anticipation with which He longs for the day when He will return and claim the Gathering of His People to be with them forever. Right now He is preparing her: "clothing" the Church in the attitudes, worship, and work that He has for her. We have a responsibility to understand what that is and how the Bride is intended to be completed so she can be presented to Him and reflect His glory at the final reunion and wedding feast.

? DISCUSSION POINTS

1. Would you agree that there is much more focus on the Kingdom rather than the Church in contemporary Christian teaching? If not, please give some examples of what leads you to that conclusion. If so, share your opinion on why you feel that might be. Do you see some links to any systems of theology that would lead towards a greater emphasis on the Kingdom than the Church? Share any thoughts you have on how you think this fits in with God's Narrative.

2. Please reflect on your own journey towards caring for and loving the Body and Bride of Christ in the way that He does. Can you identify any of the main challenges for you to grow in your appreciation of the Church?

7.3 Coworkers with God

 OBJECTIVES OF THIS TUTORIAL

In this tutorial we ask how we can be equipped to play a role in the Church's growth and development. We will also discuss how it might be possible to evaluate effectiveness and develop strategies without becoming judgmental, or reducing the wonderful mystery of the Church to formulas.

Last Time

We reminded ourselves that God is personally invested in relating to His image-bearers, as individuals and as groups. This was shown by His commitment to a personal relationship with His chosen people, Israel, despite their frequent unfaithfulness that grieved Him deeply. During our time, the primary relationship He is pursuing on the earth is with the Church. Going beyond the level of metaphor, He describes His connection with the Church as the *Head* to His *Body*. He helps us feel something of His love for the Church deeply through the image/reality of Him as the *Bridegroom* and the Church as the *Bride* He has paid for so dearly and longs to be reunited with forever. He invites us to contribute in the construction of His Building, the nourishment and growth of His Body and the preparation of His Bride.

Being equipped for our role

Our purpose in developing these resources - and we know that your purpose in studying them - is to help you be better equipped for contributing to what God is doing in and through His Church. In the last two tutorials, as we reminded ourselves of the three primary pictures of the Church He has used in His Narrative, we touched very briefly on the implications for us. If He is inviting us to be His co-workers in building His living Temple, then we need an increasing familiarity with His blueprint so we can work alongside Him with care and skill. If, as the Head of the Church, He wants to involve us in the process of fitting together, nourishing, and bringing His Body to maturity, then we need a growing sense of what health and productivity looks like for *the* Church, or *a* church. If we are to accept the great honor of helping to prepare His Bride for Him, then we need to be developing an appreciation and intuitive feel for the Church's needs that He has.

Knowing Him

So, how do we grow in clarity, appreciation and an intuitive feel for the way Jesus views His Church? Well, first of all, because He is the wise Architect, the all-powerful Head and loving Bridegroom of the Church, our capacity for the right kind of contribution depends on how well we know Him. Our perfect example, of course, is the relationship that Jesus Himself had with His Father when He was on earth. He told the Father, just before His death, that He was sending all His disciples out into the world in the same way that He had been sent, and that He'd be *in us* in the same way that the Father is *in Him*. Jesus' close relationship with the Father and the Spirit in eternity and on the earth guaranteed that He fully understood and was invested in the purpose for which He came/was sent. He has promised that He is always with us, and so as we experience walking and collaborating with Him, our minds, intuition, will and hearts are increasingly aligned to His view of His much loved Church.

Through His Narrative

A second, very related, avenue through which we grow in appreciation for how the Lord is building, nourishing and preparing His Church, is His written Narrative. If you have already completed Modules 1 and 2 (in Biblical Foundations), you will know that we use the terminology of "Narrative" to highlight the fact that God has revealed Himself through the Story of how He has interacted with His Creation...with the human race. Even though we do find many propositional statements in *Scripture*, and even though we can distil the Truth we find there into helpful doctrinal systems, it's *Him* that we need to first be looking for there. When we turn to His Word to equip ourselves as Christ's co-workers, it is with the intention of being more closely aligned with His values through the experience of observing what has motivated and directed God's words and actions down through history.

One of the ways that God equips us through His Narrative to work with understanding and empathy is through the stories of people who have known Him and glimpsed what He was doing in the world during their time. We can see Abraham's walk of faith and how God drew him into His plans to establish a nation for His global purposes. We see others who also played their part, like Isaac, Jacob and Joseph. And there is such a wealth of insights to be gleaned from seeing how God recruited and worked closely with Moses in relating to and guiding the Israelites, and Aaron as they entered the land promised by God, then later, the judges. And of course the kings, most notably David, ... and also the prophets.

But obviously, in our quest to be better equipped as Jesus' co-workers in His great work of building, guiding and preparing His Church, the most directly relevant examples are those men and women He enlisted to be involved at its beginning. As we look back from our vantage point in history at Jesus relating to His followers during the years of His ministry on earth, we can see how He was preparing them for their pivotal roles ahead. We are able to observe their growing clarity and commitment to the Body after the Spirit's promised arrival at Pentecost…how they were willing to risk everything to see people added, also their unity and common bonds as followers of the resurrected Messiah.

Then the outward thrust, the moving out beyond Jerusalem and Judea, and the dawning realization of the great scope of God's plans for His Ecclesia. This received a huge added impetus after the conversion of the young firebrand Pharisee, Paul, who would prove to have such clarity and commitment to the Cause of the Lord Jesus. Luke's, often first-hand, Acts account allows us to observe Paul and his co-workers willing to sacrifice security and comfort as they traveled widely through their part of the world, planting new local fellowships and taking the responsibility of seeing them grow to maturity. As we engage with the letters that Paul, Peter, James, John and Jude wrote to individuals and local groups of believers, God's Spirit is eager to equip us with Truth, provide us with a legitimate basis for our authority as Jesus' co-workers, and change us so we can live out the values that the apostles received directly from Him.

The Church in history

Another source of information, education and even transformation for us as servants of the Lord and His Church is the example of others down through history, since the time of the apostles. In a very real sense this is God's ongoing Narrative that is still being written in the story of the lives of His people. As God's Word itself clearly states, His specific revelation that has been preserved within the 66 books of the Bible is complete…there's no new truth to be added. But God has continued to demonstrate His amazing power, wisdom and grace as His people have given themselves wholeheartedly to be involved in His great Temple building project. When we have opportunity to hear the stories of how He has worked with weak, flawed, very human co-workers like us to achieve some amazing things, it inspires us to make ourselves available as well. We also have the opportunity to learn from the things they have attempted that have proven to be effective or otherwise.

Evaluating effectiveness

But this last point, about evaluating effectiveness, raises a critical question, or rather, a range of questions, as we consider our own contribution to His purposes. As far as efforts to see a church grow, mature and be fruitful OR when it comes to initiatives to plant a new church:

- How do we evaluate effectiveness?
- Is it possible to define any universals given the nearly infinite range of contexts and circumstances in which church work can happen?
- Does having a plan mean that God is no longer leading us?
- Is it even appropriate to think in terms of objectives, effectiveness and strategies when it relates to the Body and Bride of Christ?
- Can we take any steps to be more effective ourselves, without being judgmental or disparaging the enormous sacrifices others have made for the Lord and His Church?

These and other related questions are legitimate. We do not want to take an approach that is simplistic or reductionist…to pretend we can write formulas for something that is so complex - even on its human scale - and that ultimately rests in the infinite wisdom and love of God. We need to keep clearly in mind Paul's concern that the Colossians might become enthralled by human philosophies rather than Truth from Christ (Colossians 2:8), or that the Corinthians might be corrupted in their pure and undivided devotion to Him (2 Corinthians 11:3). Any plans or strategies we lay out must never violate the imperative of walking daily with Him and being led by His Spirit. We should be deeply appreciative of any effort or sacrifice that is made to share the Gospel and build the Lord's Ecclesia, and never allow ourselves to take a judgmental, superior stance towards His servants.

But as we've noted through the Narrative a number of times, when God created us in His image, it was with the whole range of capacities that reflect His: intellect, will, emotions, etc. And His Spirit lives in us to help us use those fully to worship and serve God. The partnership that He calls us into in the building of His Church is a genuine one. So if we're walking in dependence on Him and truly seeking to know Him and to understand His Truth, we can and should use our minds to consider what is productive and what isn't. Taking the correct stance of humility and appreciation, we can evaluate the effectiveness of strategies that have been used by other church propagators and cultivators down through history, to learn from their mistakes and seek to emulate their successes. We can look at what has lasted and ask ourselves why. And we can look at current approaches and glean from what is proving to be effective.

Vision, passion, clarity, commitment

In our daily lives and every area of human initiative - whether it's exploration, scientific discoveries, medicine, technological advances, even sport - we know that nothing worthwhile is ever achieved without a lot of dedicated, focused effort. That is just the way it is: the way God has set things up as the Great Author/Creator. If anything significant is going to be done well, it takes an individual (or more usually a team of people) with the vision, passion, detailed clarity, and willingness to do whatever it takes to see it through. Strangely though, when it comes to the enormously challenging project the Lord has invited us to be part of - building His Church (we could also describe it as seeing His Body grow to full maturity or preparing His Bride for Him), there's often a reticence from believers to apply those same principles.

As we've already highlighted in this tutorial, it is most definitely our passion and love for Jesus Christ and His Church that qualifies us to be involved in His work. In Paul's eloquent words to his friends in Corinth:

> **1 CORINTHIANS 13:2** ...if I understood all of God's secret plans and possessed all knowledge, and if I had such faith that I could move mountains, but didn't love others, I would be nothing.

But even though love is the overarching principle that must motivate our efforts, that shouldn't be seen in opposition to the pursuit of a clear vision; or asking God to guide us as we identify ways to be more effective; or even gleaning from other areas of human knowledge (e.g. linguistics, anthropology, or business principles). We should never assume that we can come close to defining everything about the glorious unfolding mystery that is the Church, but that does not mean that we should shy away from trying...in the same way that, just because we know it isn't our strength that will finally achieve anything, we shouldn't hesitate to *give it everything we've got*.

A note about Module 7

The rest of this Module (7) will be introducing and familiarizing you with a resource that helps us pursue clarity about how God works in and through His Church, and to help us chart our course towards effective contribution in His purposes.

DISCUSSION POINTS

1. Are you familiar with any tools or resources that attempt to lay out a Biblical view of what Church growth and development look like?

2. In general, have you tended to see sharing your faith with others as part of the work of *The Church* or *a church,* or is it more your own individual witness? Have you experienced being part of any concerted, planned effort of a church to reach out to those who don't know Jesus as Saviour? If so, were you (and others) equipped as part of that effort?

3. How would you describe your current role as part of your own local church? Has anyone talked specifically with you about that and guided your involvement? Do you currently have a way of evaluating how effective you are being in your contribution?

4. If you were to visit a country which missionaries had come to a few generations ago, what would you be looking for to help understand how effective their work had been? OR, would you feel it was wrong in some ways to even look from that perspective? Please explain.

7.4 Clarity in church building work

 OBJECTIVES OF THIS TUTORIAL

This tutorial discusses how systems and frameworks can be used to bring clarity to church building work as long as they are "translucent" enough to allow God's Narrative to show through clearly. It talks about the enormous and complex challenge before us and how important it is to be able to measure progress in the way God sees it.

Last time

We asked *how* we could be equipped to play a role in the Church's growth and development. We noted that first of all, we need to keep growing in our knowledge of the Lord Himself by walking with Him daily and learning more about Him through His Narrative. We see how He related to His servants under the Old Covenant, how Jesus related to His disciples, and how the apostles and early believers were led by the Spirit as they began building the Church. We can also glean from others down through history who've sacrificed and given so much for the sake of the Lord, the Gospel and His Body. We also discussed how it might be possible to evaluate effectiveness and develop strategies without becoming judgmental, or reducing the wonderful mystery of the Church to formulas.

Narrative-based frameworks

As you'll know very clearly if you've completed any of the Biblical Foundations modules, we believe that God intends us to see His written Word from a "Narrative" perspective. In other words, relating to the Bible as His Account of His actions and interactions with His Creation - most importantly with His image-bearing human race. This Narrative forms one complete and coherent *Body of Truth* - God's true description of reality - that can only be truly understood if Jesus Christ is in focus; each part points to Him and He makes sense of the whole. This perspective does not negate doctrinal systems or theological frameworks, but we treat them with great caution and always try to see "through" and "beyond" them to the *Biblical Narrative*. We're highlighting this view of God's Word one more time here because we are about to present a tool or resource that is a conceptual framework not actually present in the Narrative. We want to recognise right up front that we don't believe that any systems we come up with - no matter how well thought through or "Biblical" - should ever eclipse God's own Narrative.

But why do we need any kind of tool like this - a framework or model... whatever we might like to call it? We have the Bible, we have the book of Acts and the Epistles, shouldn't that be enough? Why do we need any kind of theoretical framework anyway?

We all have some picture in mind

Well, for one thing, we need to realize that all of us already have ideas about the Church and the part we can play in it. Even if those thoughts are not well-formed or something we can write out in bulleted points, we will all have some picture in our minds of *the Church*, and *a church* and related things like: the role of God's Word, how a church should interact with the community, what should go on in a church, and how it should be reaching out, just to name a few. Our views will have been formed by a whole network of factors: our own formative experiences, gifts and abilities, even our preferences; also our interactions and relationships; then there's the specific teaching we've heard, the reading we've done, the websites we've looked at, etc.

So again, the point we're making here is that even if we don't have a carefully defined stance we can articulate, there's an inbuilt flaw in saying, "Oh, I'm not into all that theory about the church, how it grows and matures, how churches should be planted and so on. I just read the Bible, go to Church to worship, and witness to anyone who's interested." Well, we can of course do that, but what we have to recognise is that that approach - a common one - is itself built on many assumptions. In other words, there's no way to avoid having a perspective on these important issues, it's just a matter of how closely it lines up with God's Word. We're not saying that we can have it all neatly defined or that we have to have everything pinned down before getting involved in God's purposes. Not at all! This is a journey that we're all on towards understanding and effectiveness. It's not all about formulas and theories - it's about living out His love for His Body and for the World. But just as Jesus was "full of grace and truth", for us to love the Church and others on His terms, we should be asking Him to help us find ways to align our perspective with His Truth so that we can be part of effective efforts by His Body to grow, develop and share that Truth effectively with others. And this framework we're going to share is just intended to help us in the journey, to point the way forward perhaps, but in no way to be more than it is, or to replace His Narrative. But because we already have assumptions, it's important to have some help in stepping back and evaluating which ones align with His Truth and which ones don't.

The greatest challenge there is

Another reason it is necessary for us to keep working towards greater clarity - and this tool we'll present can help with that - is because of the complexity of what faces us. It is very important for us to recognise the fact that in the entire universe, in all of Creation, there is no more important or more challenging thing that humans can be involved in than building, nurturing and extending the Church. Please, hear what we're saying here. We are not trying to make this an academic exercise, or to say that everyone involved has to be superhuman or super-saints. As Paul reminded his friends in Corinth, God delights in calling and using people in His purposes who might not be highly visible in the community as intellectually brilliant, dynamic or powerful (1 Corinthians 1:26). In fact, it's against the backdrop of human weakness that His power can be seen most clearly (2 Corinthians 12:9). So by saying that this Task He's called us to is incredibly complex and challenging, we're definitely not saying that a fruitful contribution depends on our cleverness or abilities.

But here's the thing - God wants us to make ourselves entirely available for His use - a "living sacrifice" was the vivid image Paul used (Romans 12:1) - and that includes our minds as well as our mouths, feet, hands, time, money, energy, gifts, etc. The fact that a sovereign God can use a child to share Truth with someone doesn't mean that we are excused for being childish or sloppy about His work. Just because the Good News at heart is a simple message, we mustn't take a simplistic view of the challenges involved in communicating Truth. People have been saved by reading something they found lying in the gutter, but none of us would feel that our responsibilities to the community can be fulfilled by dropping scraps of verses around the streets.

There is a prevalent viewpoint that downplays the challenge that has always faced believers and the Church in fulfilling the Task given to it by the Lord. Generally this shows up as passive carelessness, but there's also quite often an active resistance to anything that brings greater definition or implies more responsibility. This ignores the reality of what God's Word tells us about the extent to which the human race has fallen; the depth of darkness and deceit in which Satan has trapped people; the challenges faced by the early Church; the experiences of God's servants down through history; and the evidence of what we can observe in ourselves and around us. All of this adds up overwhelmingly to the conclusion that this is, in fact, an enormously complex and difficult challenge we face. Acknowledging this should not lead us to despair. It should make us want an even closer connection with the Head of the Church...and along with that a desire to understand the challenge better and to use all of our abilities and whatever tools we can, to help us head in the right direction and stay on track.

Measuring progress

One result of something being so complex and challenging is that it is often difficult to evaluate progress. How can I know that what I've done today has really contributed to God's purposes? How can I be confident that I'm not involved in things just because I enjoy or feel comfortable doing them? What mileposts can we use as we look back or project forward? How do we define "growth" or "progress" in relation to a church? What does health and fruitfulness look like from the perspective of the Head of the Church? Is there any appropriate way to measure *results* or should we only be interested in the *process*?

Unless we've considered carefully and described adequately how God intends for His Church to expand, grow, multiply and mature, our tendency will be to measure progress in superficial ways. Our default is to look for the outer *form*, the tangible things like church attendance, size and quality of buildings, dollars in the offering plate or even programs that are running each week. In another kind of ministry it can become books sold, clicks on websites, the number of 'likes' or 'follows'. With our personal evangelism we might focus on how many people we've witnessed to or been able to bring along to church. If we're involved in cross-cultural church planting we may count how many teams are out there, socio-economic programs, people groups who've been "engaged", cell groups established, or even translation projects underway.

Now we're NOT saying that any of those things in themselves are bad: in fact, they might represent a real cause for gratitude and be one of the ways we measure effectiveness and progress. But if we're preoccupied with these more tangible signposts we can mistake them for the goal itself, and fail to do what Paul described to the believers in Philippi - to "press on to reach the end of the race and receive the heavenly prize for which God, through Christ Jesus, is calling us." And even in the short term, if we confine ourselves to very limited categories for gaugeing results, we can fail to recognise the amazing things that God is doing through and around us. Also, if we have unchallenged assumptions about what progress will look like, it's almost inevitable that we'll unconsciously direct our energy and resources towards outcomes that may not be the things that God sees as most important.

You don't need many conversations with people or to read lots of books or check out many websites to realize that there are a lot of different perspectives out there about the Church. There are endless ideas, strategies, models and programs, some of them developed for specific contexts and others with more universal aspirations. It can be overwhelming and confusing trying to sort through them all. The last thing we want to do is add yet another one. Instead, what we hope to present is something that is more fundamental, something that actually helps us assess different approaches and come to conclusions about whether they move us toward God's purposes in and through the Church or not. Having said that, we recognise that the way we describe things, the issues that we give prominence to, even the categories we choose, all represent some theological and methodological conclusions… that's impossible to avoid, and we don't want to pretend that we can find some neutral, detached place to stand and describe these things. In fact, if we are not passionate about and committed to these things, then we probably shouldn't be talking about them. But our hope is that what we present is actually founded in His divine being, it accurately traces threads from His Narrative, and that it helps us project those out into real-life contexts in valid and helpful ways.

Another reason why it is very helpful for us to have some defined categories for our work with the Church is simply to give us shared terminology. We accept that when we use a word or phrase in a conversation, we never have 100% correlation of meaning, but if we've defined those terms together previously then we have a much greater chance of communication. We don't have to start from scratch and redefine terms every time we want to talk…that is what words and language do. And so when we're talking about something as complex and challenging as all the different aspects of the work that relates to the Church, and churches, it is valuable to know we've previously agreed on some definitions and broad categories.

Read the article below and then discuss the following questions.

....

Success or failure in tough soil

We're sitting in the house on the ridge looking out over the dry mountains, sparsely covered with stunted pines and fir trees. We flew in a few days ago and landed on the crazy airstrip at the head of the canyon…we've seen other strips that are steeply sloped, but this one also had a significant sideways bend in the middle! We're visiting a couple who moved from another country to live in this area about 6 years before. Ufa and Ilke (not their real names) have learned the national language and then the minority language of these people who grow their crops - often illegal drugs - wherever they can in the stony red earth. It hasn't been easy to become part of this community spread out in little hamlets. After experiencing tyranny in one form or another for generations, the people are understandably suspicious of outsiders. But through patience, kindness and practical help, and now being comfortable in the language that's spoken around the fires in homes, Ufa and Ilke have gradually won trust and built real friendships.

As we talk with them now though, they wonder out loud if the six years have really been worth it. It was the vision of planting a church in this very needy area that brought them, but they can hardly say that has happened. There have been some real blows, many disappointments. A number of friends have died in alcohol-fueled violence. There are ongoing feuds between clans, and abuse in families is rife. So what can we see that God has done? Well, there's the guy they pay to bring firewood and do some work around the place. He's a believer now and has gradually separated out from the worst aspects of the culture. Now he's trying to share his faith with his wife. Oh, and there's the teenage girl who lives just over there on the next ridge…she too is now saved and comes around two or three times a week to study the Bible. She has been taking food regularly to the only other believer, a crippled older man who loves to sit in the sun outside his hut and talk about Jesus with anyone who comes by. But there's no church to see for six years of effort.

Or is there? Sure, it might be a stretch to claim there's a full-blown church functioning in this community, but how should we measure the relative value of what God has done, what He's allowed Ufa and Ilke to be part of? Now, including the two of them, there are five children of God here, all of whom speak the language of the community. Ilke has made a start on translating God's Word into that language. They have made mp3s of Ufa sharing from God's Narrative which all three believers listen to regularly and sometimes play for others to hear. They are seeing understanding and gradual changes in the lives of all three. There's a feeling of something in common between them, even a growing sense of responsibility to share the Good News about Jesus with their community. The young girl's care for the old crippled man to whom she is not related is unheard of. And the other middle-aged man is trying to be patient with his wife even when she is drunk and mocks him for his faith.

So is there really nothing happening? How do we measure success? The value of sacrifice, disappointments and patient effort? Most importantly, how does God measure success? How does this line up with who God is? And Him creating beings in His image? His redemptive purposes after the Fall? With Him building His Church, leading His Body, preparing His Bride? When we measure by that scale, rather than by the tangibles like numbers, buildings and programs, surely a great deal is going on. What a privilege to be here. To witness first-hand the small, frail beginnings of what God is doing in this very unpromising soil.

We fly out the next day, knuckles white as we hold straps as the 5 seat aircraft bounces down the gravel runway, finally struggling its way into the air meters before the 3,000-foot drop at the end. Four months later we get an email to say that the wife of the one guy is now saved…then later his grown son. Two years later we hear that there's a small group of about 20 believers meeting regularly. They get together at the hut of the crippled man so he doesn't have to walk on the steep slopes. A couple of the men are beginning to teach God's Word to their own people. While Ufa and Ilke are away for six months in their home country, people from a cult that's sprung up in the regional capital come through trying to entice the believers with promises of prosperity. But they stand firm and send them away, "Our lives are tough but we have received the unbelievable wealth of God's grace."

Twenty believers meeting in a ramshackle hut after nine years of work? What scale will we use to measure that as a success or failure?

CLARITY IN CHURCH BUILDING WORK

> **? DISCUSSION POINTS**
>
> **1.** Honestly trying to put yourself in Ufa and Ilke's situation do you think you would consider that it had been worth it? Do you think you'd be tempted to wonder if it wasn't God's will for you to be there?
>
> **2.** Do you think there would be a point at which you could legitimately say that it was time to consider moving on? How do you think you would go about making that decision? What would you be basing it on?
>
> **3.** Do you think that a church (a true New Testament ecclesia) could have been said to exist at the six-year point when the story begins? What about after nine years when the story ends? What are you basing your perspective on? Please explain.

7.5 Word. Identity. Life. Discipleship.

✓ OBJECTIVES OF THIS TUTORIAL

This tutorial gives an introduction to the W.I.L.D. outline in the form of 20 questions - five in each of the areas of Word, Identity, Life and Discipleship. We will look how it can be used, and also reflect on the fact that when we look at how Truth is producing life, growth and fruit in a person or a group of people, we are talking about a process - a journey - not a completed product or destination. We will discuss how W.I.L.D. is a way of describing the primary threads in God's Word that start with His own Being, run through His interactions as Creator with His creation, tie together in the person of Christ, and reach out to the Church.

Last time

We discussed how systems and frameworks could be used to bring clarity to Church building work as long as they are "translucent" enough to allow God's Narrative to show through clearly. The Bible *is* enough, but that does not absolve us from the responsibility of using our minds and every resource that God "sanctifies" and provides us with to be better equipped for His work.

Whether we know it or not, we all have an existing picture of the Church and our part in it, and we are responsible to ask God to show us whether or not that picture is aligned with Truth. We need a clear view of the enormous and complex challenge before us so we can commit fully to the right kind of response.

We also need to consider ways to measure progress in the way God sees it so we don't default to using only tangible factors and shaping our work accordingly. And having terminology and agreed-upon categories helps us talk about the complex challenge.

W.I.L.D. (Word. Identity. Life. Discipleship.)

The W.I.L.D. framework you'll find here is designed to help our understanding of how Truth produces life, growth and fruit. It could be expressed in any number of ways; for example, it could be stated in terms of commitments or vision: "We are committed to giving people access to…" "Our vision is to see people growing in…" The version below takes the approach of considering each point with a particular person or a group in mind, and so we have put it in the form of questions. There are many implicit ideas embedded in these questions and we have fleshed those out much more fully in the following tutorials in Module 7.

We have tried to introduce the questions in a form that does not immediately limit their application. We have used "they" and "their" so the questions can refer to individuals or groups generally, or to a person or a church more specifically. There is something of a dilemma in doing that though, because an individual believer's growth and fruitfulness is never completely separate from relationships with other believers and particularly with a church that is growing and fruitful. And so even though these questions could pertain to a person or a few individuals who come to faith on their own, there is an inbuilt assumption that they will at some point become part of a local *ecclesia* - a church.

You'll see too that we have purposely used language that describes this as an ongoing process ("Are they learning to…" "Are they increasingly able to…") It is not our intention to present a picture/model of the perfect convert or church, because we know those don't exist. Each individual and body of believers - indeed the whole Body of Christ - is on a journey towards the time when He will bring all things finally into what He intends. So when we are evaluating, defining a vision, or determining directions, what we are looking for are signs that Truth is at work and that things are on a trajectory towards what God intends.

WORD

- Are they able to access the Bible in a form that clearly and faithfully communicates God's revelation to them?
- Are they having God's Word presented to them in a way that allows it to enter and engage their hearts at a worldview level?
- Are they learning to give God's Word its proper place and authority?
- Are they growing in their ability to correctly understand God's Word as His complete Narrative, with Jesus Christ as the heart of the story and its interpretive key?
- Are they increasingly able to make use of God's Word as He intends for His children and His Church?

IDENTITY

- Are they increasingly clear about - and able to articulate - their true identity from God's perspective?
- Are they learning to see their story embedded in the larger Narrative of the Church, stretching back to Pentecost and forward to Christ's return?
- Are they growing in their understanding of the bonds that unite them to the global/local Body under Christ as its Head?
- Are they learning to view others according to truth, and rejecting the divisions, biases and tensions that often define the wider society?
- Are they growing in their understanding of how to appropriately represent the Lord in their current spheres of contact and in others He might lead them to be involved in?

LIFE

- Are they experiencing a deepening relationship with Jesus, learning to depend more completely on Him in different areas of their lives, and gradually seeing their values and behavior change as a result?
- Are they gaining clarity about the true purpose for which they exist, and are they increasingly able to identify those things that hinder their life in Christ?
- Are they increasingly able to make good decisions based on their understanding of God's local and global purposes, and to use their time, money and other resources accordingly?
- Are they learning to shape the *form* of what they do to serve whatever *function* they are convinced will lead to the *fulfillment* of God's objectives?
- Are they growing in their commitment to reproducing the life they have in Christ, are they equipped with the resources and skills to do so, and are they prioritizing opportunities where there is real need and hunger?

DISCIPLESHIP

- Are they seeing all other ties, loyalties and commitments being increasingly defined by their primary relationship; disciples of their Master, Jesus Christ?
- Are they being helped to apply the general truth from God's Word to their own specific real-life situations?

WORD. IDENTITY. LIFE. DISCIPLESHIP.

- Are they able to access regular, godly input and genuine friendships that intentionally help them along as they follow Jesus in the walk of faith?

- Are they being encouraged to function in the areas in which God has gifted and given them abilities so they can develop in their service to Him and His Body?

- Do they have access to defined pathways that offer Bible-based resources, practical instruction and relational discipleship to adequately equip them to serve the church locally and globally?

Why in this order?

The order of the four categories - Word, Identity, Life and Discipleship - has been carefully considered. Even though, as we'll discuss shortly, these areas don't function at all independently in real life, there is still a kind of progression in terms of which is more foundational than the next.

It's obvious that the entrance and engagement of God's Word in the life of an individual or a group is a prerequisite to anything else happening. We will talk about this more in later Module 7 tutorials. Without the communication of truth, and then God's Spirit working with that truth to generate a response, nothing else happens; no faith, growth or fruit can exist. So putting the communication and response to God's Word as our first area we look at to evaluate what is happening with a person, or with a group of people, is a fairly straightforward choice.

But why then do we have *Identity* next? Again, we'll be going further into the whole area of Identity elsewhere, but we see this area as foundational for any growth or fruitfulness in the life of an individual or group. In fact, before life can even begin (i.e. the new birth) someone needs to glimpse who they actually are as they stand before a holy, righteous Creator. Then, real growth happens in our lives only as we begin to understand who God says we now are: new creations, in Christ, His cherished children, members of His Body, etc. And fruit is produced, as we understand who we are in relation to Him and to others.

So what next? *Discipleship* could possibly have come next because it is about the relationships that purposefully encourage growth and fruit. But the area we've called *Life* seems even more foundational, in that it considers the quality and shape the new life is taking, or if it even exists. As we think about ourselves, or someone we are sharing God's Word with, or a small group, or a church, what we hope to see is evidence of true life that God's Spirit is producing through His Word. We're looking for changes and activities that are the natural outflow of life that only *the Life* gives.

Why these particular four areas?

We're not claiming any kind of inspiration for this W.I.L.D. framework. There are other helpful resources that have been developed for evaluating personal Christian development, church planting, church growth, etc., that are useful and well worth looking at. It would have been possible to use different names, more, or less categories, and so on. But after a lot of thought, a number of refinements, and widespread use over a number of years in many contexts, it has proven to be an effective way of talking about the complex and challenging topic of how God's Word produces life, growth and fruit in individuals and communities. And, not without merit, is the fact that WILD forms a nice mnemonic to help us remember it by.

God's essential being

But the real validity of focusing on these four areas doesn't stem from how helpful they are, even though we obviously believe that valid things should have useful applications in the real world. Their real validity comes from the fact that they describe threads that are tied into the self-existence of God:

- God speaks, He communicates truly (*Word*).
- God is a Three-In-One-God, perfect unity in diversity (*Identity*).
- God is completely Alive, He *is* Life (*Life*).
- God loves fully, He *is* Love (*Discipleship*).

The Creator

They also reflect God's relationship as Creator to us, His image bearers, as we see consistently in His Narrative:

- He communicates Truth to us (*Word*).
- He relates to us consistently as Author, Creator, Father, Righteous Judge, Redeemer, etc. (*Identity*).
- He gives us physical life and offers us spiritual life through the new birth (*Life*).
- He loves the world, and has a special love for those He calls His own (*Discipleship*).

The Son

They can be further traced to God's Son, the Lord Jesus Christ:

- He is *the Word* who revealed God in the form of a human being. He said, "I am the Truth" (*Word*).
- He is completely God and completely man but without contradiction. He is the Servant King (*Identity*).
- He said "I am the Life", and He showed us how to live out God's life without being corrupted by sin and death (*Life*).
- He is the great Discipler and Shepherd who gave His life for the sheep (*Discipleship*).

The Ecclesia (Church)

And we see the threads continuing on in the way He designed and developed His Body:

- The Spirit who "leads into all Truth" came. Through gifted individuals (prophets/apostles) God completed His revelation. The Church is entrusted with treasuring, safeguarding and sharing His Word (*Word*).
- The Church is called His Temple, His Body, His Bride…and shares an identity for all eternity with Jesus. All believers are made members when they are born again (*Identity*).
- The Church has no life apart from Him. It serves as His physical Body on earth by living out His values, and by being His "hands", "feet" and "mouth" in the world (*Life*).
- As the Head, He has absolute authority. He sent His Church out to make new disciples and teach them all His Truth (*Discipleship*).

? **DISCUSSION POINTS**

1. What is your initial response to the 20 questions in the W.I.L.D. outline above? Are there any that are not clear? Do you think you would benefit from asking these questions about yourself? (Take a moment to go through and replace "they" and "their" with "I" and "my" etc.)

2. Go through those 20 questions and change them into statements that begin with something like, "I want to help people to learn/be able to/experience, etc...." As you describe that kind of contribution, share anything you care to about how well equipped you currently feel to do that and any specific areas that you would like to learn more about or to grow more in.

7.6 Access to the Bible

> ✓ **OBJECTIVES OF THIS TUTORIAL**
>
> This tutorial discusses the first question in the area of *Word*: 'Are they able to access the Bible in a form that clearly and faithfully communicates God's revelation to them?'

Last time

We looked at the W.I.L.D. outline in the form of 20 questions - five in each of the different areas of Word, Identity, Life and Discipleship. We discussed that it can be used in a number of different ways but we chose this form so as not to limit its application; also to reflect the fact that when we look at how Truth is producing life, growth and fruit in a person or in a group of people, we are talking about a process - a journey - not a completed product or destination. We also shared some thoughts on the *order* of the four categories: How the entrance of God's *Word* is the first in order because it changes who we are, then clarity about *Identity* is foundational to *Life* changes, etc.

Finally we asked why we chose these four areas specifically… and reflected on the fact that while they are not "inspired" they are a very appropriate way of describing the primary threads in God's Word that start with His own Being, run through His interactions as Creator with His creation, tie together in the person of Christ, and reach out to the Church.

A reminder - the "W" in W.I.L.D.

In the next few tutorials we want to look further into the area of *Word* and how it relates to the life, growth and fruit of a person/group/church. Here again are the five questions that we proposed asking when we considered the first area - Word - in our W.I.L.D. categories. There is a lot of implicit stuff embedded in each of these questions, so we're going to go through and consider each of them in turn, starting with this first (underlined) question.

- <u>Are they able to access the Bible in a form that clearly and faithfully communicates God's revelation to them?</u>

- Are they having God's Word presented to them in a way that allows it to enter and engage their hearts at a worldview level?
- Are they learning to give God's Word its proper place and authority?
- Are they growing in their ability to correctly understand God's Word as His complete Narrative, with Jesus Christ as the heart of the story and its interpretive key?
- Are they increasingly able to make use of God's Word as He intends for His children and His Church?

God communicates

In any attempt we make to describe God, the fact that He communicates must feature very prominently. Even that we know He exists at all is clear evidence of this. Just because many human beings have an opinion, born from their limited, fallen, perspective, about what *they* feel would be a compelling form of communication from God, doesn't change things even slightly. The fact is, He has revealed Himself in the best possible ways to get through and tell us what we need to know. As we've noted many times, and as His own Word attests, the universe we live in is a form of His communication to human beings that never stops (Romans 1:20). But the primary way He has communicated of course, as the opening words of the book of Hebrews say, is through the prophets: through His thoughts that have been expressed in human sounds, words, sentences and paragraphs and written down by His specially gifted servants. But now, in this final stage of His great Narrative, "He has spoken to us through His Son" (Hebrews 1:2).

An astounding thing to note is that God's communication is always representative of His grace. No one, individually or collectively, deserves to have God speak to them. Communication, language, speech, discourse; these are all a gift from God to us as His image-bearing race. This connection between communication and grace as essential qualities of His being are highlighted against the backdrop of human sin and corruption. This was the case down through Old Testament history, as it is today. And just like everything else about God, where this is revealed to us most clearly and understandably is in the Incarnation, in Jesus Christ. He, the living expression of God, came to the world, lived in a human form that didn't set him apart in any way, lived within a particular cultural setting, spoke a language with human vocal chords. Why? Because God takes it on Himself to give us *access* to truth, to His revelation. He takes on Himself the burden of communication.

More than just available

So our question about whether someone has *access* to God's Communication stems from this source. We see overwhelming evidence all the way through God's Narrative that He desires people to have full access to His Word, and that because of His grace He takes it on Himself to provide a way for them to have that access. His commitments go far beyond simply making information *available* so that someone somewhere might find out about Him if they try hard enough, or happen to belong to some privileged group. But this also intersects with another essential part of God's character: He draws human beings into real partnerships with Himself in His purposes. As well as being the God who communicates and a God of grace, He is also the God who *equips* and *sends*. In our present time of history defined by the New Covenant, He has chosen His Body, His Church and its members - us - as the means by which His Communication is to be made accessible.

So when we are involved in giving a friend, a group of people, a community, or a whole people group real access to God's revelation, we are participating in something that flows directly from the being of God Himself. As His chosen hands, feet, mouths, minds and hearts on earth, He wants us to be committed to providing real access to Him and His Truth in the way Jesus was when He gladly gave up His divine rights to become a human being, to serve and to die for that purpose. Providing people with access always involves a cost for those who provide it. That's why it's linked directly to God's grace. The further we're willing to go in this, the more the cost. Down through history servants of God and His Church have paid the price by giving up their careers, their ambitions and even their lives. Others have been willing to give their finances to support the efforts of others. But often the cost is in less dramatic or obvious ways, and there are a million reasons to stop at different points along the way...perfectly good, sensible, rational reasons.

Our first W.I.L.D. question links *access* to the issue of an individual or group being able to engage with the Bible "in a form that clearly and faithfully communicates" to them. This obviously leads us to talk about language. Even if I know the book in my hotel room is a Bible, it's hardly available, much less accessible, to me if it's in a language I don't speak at all. So the question would be relatively simple to answer if it was just a matter of determining which languages someone speaks, or if there's a Bible translation in a given language.

Hopefully we agree that God's commitment to providing access to His revelation means that individuals, communities and churches should be able to read the Bible in a language they are familiar with. We can even go further than this and talk about optimum access through "heart" language, the language of the home, the language in which people conceptualize their worldview, the language in which they pass on their beliefs from one generation to another. But to really do justice to this subject we'd have to consider a whole web of related issues such as the role of language domains, bilingualism, and links between culture and language, just to name a few. These topics are investigated in more depth elsewhere in the *AccessTruth Curriculum* (Communication Foundations) and so we won't dig into them here.

Of course this first question should be fairly easy to answer if we're talking about any of the estimated 209 million people from the 2000 languages without a Bible translation in the world. But how does our initial W.I.L.D. question relate to a context such as the UK, USA or Australia where translations have been available in the dominant language, English, for many generations? Well for one thing, it is more than obvious that English is not the first language for many of the people we meet at work, at school, selling us fuel at the service station or coming into our churches. As an example, in Australia over a quarter of residents were born overseas; 20% of the population prefer to speak a language other than English at home; nearly half a million people don't speak English.

So whether it's someone we've been building a friendship with at work, a new couple who've been attending a Bible study…if we're evaluating the outreach ministries of our church, or thinking about an appropriate witness to migrant workers in an Asian city, the dynamics are obviously different but the basic questions about access to God's revelation are very similar. We are not trying to draw hard and fast conclusions or make a list of rules. What we are considering together is categories and principles that tie into God's character and flow through His Narrative to evaluate our involvement (current or future) in building His Temple, nourishing His Body and equipping His Bride.

Providing real access

You'll notice that the question we initially asked refers to "a form that clearly and faithfully communicates…" Here there's an obvious application to new Bible translation projects. In Module 8 of the *AccessTruth Curriculum*, we present an introduction to the translators' challenge of clearly and faithfully transferring meaning from one language to another. In other words, from the original Hebrew and Greek texts in which the prophets and apostles wrote God's Word to a "receptor" or "target" language. But these principles are also relevant to the issue of English versions and very pertinent as we consider real access in any situation. It's not only transfer of meaning from one recognized language to another we have to consider when we're thinking about sharing God's Word with someone, but also their culture, generation, social status, education, etc. All of these things relate to our commitment to share His Communication clearly with them. We'll discuss this more extensively when we tackle the next W.I.L.D. question that goes beyond the *form* of an accessible Bible into the effective presentation of Truth at a worldview level.

Finally, a few more thoughts about the *form* in which people encounter God's Word. We believe that it's significant that God gave us a lasting *written* record of the words, sentences, paragraphs, books and letters that He has preserved as the canon of Scripture. In Module 8 we'll present a much more in-depth argument for the enormous benefits of literacy, for individuals and for churches. Unfortunately, some recent missiological models have tended to characterize a value for the written word and the reading and writing skills of literacy as somehow paternalistic and tied to a western logic system. These "oral communication" theories have tended to pit traditional ideas of the written Bible against "Bible Storying" which is expressed through Narrative and other indigenous forms of communication such as chanting and dance. We believe that this labeling and dichotomising is unhelpful. It is not an either or choice. Anyone sharing God's Word should be seeking to hone their skills as a story-teller. God, after all, as we've said many times, is the Divine Story-teller, the Author of the great Narrative of Creation and reality.

Our commitment to providing access should lead us to utilize every appropriate communication means available that does not distort the Message. In many contexts now that means using technology - smartphones, the internet, social media - just as in other contexts it means learning to tell God's Story in compelling natural ways or working many long hours at a computer to produce a clear and faithful translation. This was the commitment Paul was describing to his friends in Corinth when he said, "...I try to find common ground with everyone, doing everything I can to save some. I do everything to spread the Good News and share in its blessings" (1 Corinthians 9:22–23).

Some extra questions

To go along with the first question under *Word* - 'Are they able to access the Bible in a form that clearly and faithfully communicates God's revelation to them?' We can now add some extra questions:

- Does it feel as though it's God Himself speaking to them through the Bible when they hear or read it, OR does the language tend to create barriers and give the idea that it is for someone else?
- Does the language they are hearing the Truth in give them the ability to talk about it in their homes, with their friends, and in the community?
- Are they able to access God's Word in the available media and technologies that the wider society is using?

ACCESS TO THE BIBLE

❓ DISCUSSION POINTS

1. Reflect on the idea that access to Truth always costs those who provide it. Can you put into words your own personal current level of commitment to providing others access to God's Word? Are there any fears or reservations related to this?

2. What are the top 5 reasons in your view for the huge number of languages in which there is not yet a translation of God's Word?

3. Have you ever tried personally to share God's Word with someone for whom English is their second language or observed someone in that situation who attended your church or somewhere similar? Describe their level of access. (Reference the extra questions in the paragraph above to describe it if possible.)

7.7 Engaging at a worldview level

 OBJECTIVES OF THIS TUTORIAL

This tutorial discusses the second question in the area of *Word*: 'Are they having God's Word presented to them in a way that allows it to enter and engage their hearts at a worldview level?'

Last time

We reminded ourselves of the amazing fact that God is committed to communication, revelation. This is interwoven with His grace because nothing compels Him to communicate... no one earns the right to hear from God. More than simply making Truth available, He pays the cost of giving people genuine access to His Revelation of Himself. He invites us - His Body on earth - to share in this commitment and, like Him, gladly pay the cost.

We also talked about *access* in terms of how familiar an individual or a group is with the language in which they have the Bible available. This is not only relevant in cross-cultural church planting contexts but also in our own multi-cultural contexts. And finally, we thought about the need to use every available means to communicate God's Truth without distorting the Message.

The second question under "W" for *Word*

- Are they able to access the Bible in a form that clearly and faithfully communicates God's revelation to them?
- <u>Are they having God's Word presented to them in a way that allows it to enter and engage their hearts at a worldview level?</u>
- Are they learning to give God's Word its proper place and authority?
- Are they growing in their ability to correctly understand God's Word as His complete Narrative, with Jesus Christ as the heart of the story and its interpretive key?
- Are they increasingly able to make use of God's Word as He intends for His children and His Church?

This question is really an extension of the first one that we looked at in the last tutorial, although that was specifically talking about the *form* in which a person or group of people are accessing the Bible itself: i.e. the language or medium in which it's available. But now we want to consider the way God's Word is being presented to them by others, ...perhaps by *us*. Here we're looking at more than just the words, sentences and paragraphs of the Bible itself - what the Bible itself calls *inspired* or "breathed out by God". We now want to consider how a person/group is having God's inspired, unchanging and infallible written Word shared with them. Again, what we're concerned most with is their degree of real *access* to God's revelation of Truth.

All of the different Truth-sharing contexts

If we were primarily focusing here on the presentation of God's Word in the more formal, corporate setting of a church - the kind that many of us from traditional Christian backgrounds are most familiar with - then we'd be talking about *homiletics*: "the art of preaching or writing sermons". And, of course, in many contexts, what is taught from the church's pulpit is most definitely a key part of the picture. In fact, as we move on to other W.I.L.D. questions, the whole area of how people are hearing God's Word taught authoritatively within the setting of the gathered *ecclesia* will come more into focus. But for now we're starting further back and asking a more general question about *any* situation where someone is not just reading/listening to the Bible but where they are also having it presented, shared and explained to them.

Questions about the *form* in which the explanation comes to them are very similar to those we asked about the *form* of the Bible itself. If someone is not familiar with the language of the Scriptural text they are engaging with, then it will also be challenging for them to understand any additional comments that are being made about it.

Two compelling reasons to value "heart language"

As we've said, it isn't our intention in this curriculum to make pronouncements like, "Everyone should be taught in their first language." But to "put our cards on the table" as it were, we do hold "heart language" communication of Truth as an ideal that should be vigorously pursued in many contexts. For one thing, our theology leads us to understand that God places a premium on there being representation from every language/ethnic group in His Church and ultimately around His throne. His glory will shine out for eternity in all its richness because it will be seen through a multi-faceted prism that's made up of people from "every nation and tribe and people and language" praising Him. So that in itself is a very potent reason for valuing opportunities to share God's Truth with people in their own languages. Secondly, our experience and all the evidence we see leads us to conclude that a group that has had Truth consistently presented in their own language (given many other factors that are touched on in the

W.I.L.D. outline) has a greater chance of growing and bearing fruit than one that only has access through a language they've had to learn.

But given that our perspective here is wider, taking into account the whole range of possible scenarios we can consider for sharing God's Word, perhaps the way we can state this is along these lines: *God's gracious commitment to providing access is compelling motivation for us, His co-workers, to keep moving towards the best possible forms of sharing His Word with others...whatever that means in the situation.*

Unleashing its potential

Back to our question: *Are they having God's Word presented to them in a way that allows it to enter and engage their hearts at a worldview level?* When we talk about allowing God's Word to do something, we're not inferring that as humans we control its inherent power. God says that His word is like a fire and a hammer that smashes rocks to pieces (Jeremiah 23:29). Paul called the Good News about Christ (which by extension refers to the whole of God's Word that points forward and backward to Him) "the power of God at work" (Romans 1:16). Elsewhere it is said to be alive and powerful, cutting through peoples' pretenses and defenses like a super sharp sword (Hebrews 4:12). Charles Spurgeon famously likened God's Word to a lion that shouldn't so much be defended as let loose.

So when we consider how God's Word is being presented to someone, we're obviously not questioning the power of God's Word. What we're asking - to badly mix these metaphors - is whether the fire is being fanned, the power unleashed, the hammer wielded, if the sword is piercing and the lion has been let loose. This touches, as do so many things, on the mystery of how God's Sovereignty co-exists with human free will, and how God channels His infinite wisdom and power through finite, flawed human beings like us. But we know that those things do co-exist and that He sends us out as His witnesses, storytellers and disciple-makers.

Our mandate to teach

Before He left the earth, Jesus sent the disciples out - and through them all His church - with the responsibility of *teaching* disciples from all the world's ethnic groups. The Holy Spirit came and gave - and continues to give - different ones in the *Ecclesia* special abilities or gifts for specific teaching roles in different situations. Paul, writing to his young disciple and co-worker Timothy, describes himself as a preacher, apostle and teacher of the Good News. Timothy is to hold on to the good teaching he's heard from Paul, to carefully guard this treasure so it's not changed or eroded, and then to pass it on intact to other trustworthy people who will do the same (2 Timothy 1:11 - 2:2). Later, in the same letter, (2 Timothy 3:16-17), Paul describes a servant of the Church like Timothy as having the resources within God's inspired Word to teach people so that they realize where their thoughts and actions are inconsistent with Truth, so they can realign them and live as God wants, and to equip them for productive contribution in His purposes.

So when we consider a specific situation where God's Word is being shared, we need to ask ourselves if it is being done in such a way that allows its inherent power to flow freely. Does the person sharing (and that might well be us) take very seriously the responsibility and privilege? Are their own lives aligned to the Truth they are sharing? Are they gifted by God's Spirit for teaching in this particular kind of setting? Are they properly equipped and can they explain and apply it faithfully?

Our question uses three words that take us further in considering the *access* that a person or group is being given to God's Word; *enter, engage* and *worldview*. It digs down into the responsibility God gives to us as His witnesses, His Truth-bearers. It recognises that we haven't necessarily communicated just because we've said something. Even if we share a basic language with someone, we can all think of many instances in which the words we've used in a conversation have not ended up in clear communication. Of course there can be any number of reasons for confusion and misunderstandings, but one way of describing the most foundational layer in which communication does, or doesn't, happen is *worldview*.

Worldview commitments

In other parts of the *AccessTruth Curriculum* we discuss this concept of worldview in much more depth than we will here (see Tutorials 6.1 - 6.4). We utilize the following definition, by James Sire, that is slightly technical perhaps, but helpful nonetheless for our purposes here of considering whether or not the way Truth is being presented helps someone have *access* or not.

> **Worldview is a commitment, a fundamental orientation of the heart, that can be expressed as a story or in a set of presuppositions (assumptions which may be true, partially true or entirely false) that we hold (consciously or subconsciously, consistently or inconsistently) about the basic constitution of reality, and that provides the foundation on which we live and move and have our being**[1].

There are some very far-reaching implications of the reality that people don't just have certain beliefs and values in the way that someone *has* a certain hair color or a particular accent. As Sire correctly identifies, when we talk about someone's *worldview* we are talking about things they are committed to, or invested in. If a shipwreck survivor has been holding on to something grimly for days to keep themselves afloat, there's every chance they'll find it difficult to loosen their grip when a rescue boat finally arrives.

---

1   James W. Sire. The Universe Next Door: A Basic Worldview Catalog, 5th Edition. Kindle Edition. 2009

People don't easily let go of the story or explanation that they are told - by themselves, by their society, and by Satan - makes sense of everything. The fingers of their souls, so to speak, have been holding on so tightly to their worldview for so long that it is painful to even open their hand so they can let go and reach for the Truth.

These commitments are on a cognitive level (i.e. related to logic and conscious thought) but they are also emotional...as Sire says, an "orientation of the heart". It's the default direction their lives head towards like a compass needle swinging back to point north. And so people have often never stopped to analyze what it is that is really motivating and driving them to be who they are, or valuing the things that they do; they don't know, or often don't care to know, why they think, speak and act the way they do. There is a strong impulse *against* that kind of scrutiny. It's too confronting, too risky, too painful.

And this worldview that each person holds is comprehensive, in the sense that it tries to explain all of his or her experience. Human beings are created specifically to be the listeners - the active participating audience - for God's true Story of all things. Of course we are fallen and corrupted through our choice to tell our own small, false stories. But we're still created to live in this world and to have sense made of it for us. That's not at all to say that peoples' worldviews are always coherent...that they don't have many gaps and inconsistencies. They most certainly do, but the difficulty that people face is finding any ground from which to evaluate the contradictions and weaknesses. They can't take off the "glasses" of their worldview to look at themselves or anything else without it. To change the metaphor, it's like the water in which a fish swims. It has no point of reference to imagine any other way of existing.

Preparing the soil

So the first thing we should be looking for in any situation where Truth is being presented is a real commitment being made to understand the listeners' worldview. Good intentions and a passion for sharing the Truth are absolutely necessary. But a love for Christ and others and a desire to share God's Word is not in opposition to a passion for understanding people's worldview commitments and fundamental orientations. In fact, not to do so often demonstrates a lack of love and respect; a preoccupation with ourselves, with our own worldview commitments and orientation. We must be willing to listen to and understand other people's stories before we offer God's wonderful Narrative with its complete and satisfying answers that people's hearts really desire.

Secondly, if a presentation of God's Word is going to enter and engage at the deepest level, it will be in the process of the listeners questioning their worldview commitments and orientation. Far too often, for example, in their eagerness to get to the "good part"

- the Good News about Christ - servants of the Church fail to carefully prepare the soil, or rather, to wait for God's Spirit to use His Word to prepare the soil. If peoples' worldview allegiance remains solidly in place, if the alignment of their hearts isn't being challenged, if they are still holding on tightly to their own "story", then the Sword isn't penetrating, the Hammer isn't crushing the stone, and the repentance that precedes faith is not taking place.

Finally, any efforts to share Truth should be focused on bringing people to stand before God in all His glory and grace. Although different programs and strategies, apologetics and convincing arguments, testimonies and personal stories might have their place, they are only ultimately successful if people are being helped to hear God's own voice speaking to them. It is Him revealing Himself, telling them His true Story, explaining who they actually are and how they stand in His eyes, drawing their eyes towards the only solution to their true needs, His Son Jesus Christ, giving them hope and purpose… this is how Truth enters and engages at the fundamental - worldview - level and produces repentance, faith, life, growth and fruit.

Some extra questions

To go along with the question: 'Are they having God's Word presented to them in a way that allows it to enter and engage their hearts at a worldview level?' We can now add these:

- Are those sharing Truth taking the responsibility seriously; are they qualified, gifted and equipped for that particular setting, and are they genuinely committed to getting to know and understand the worldview of those they're sharing with?
- Is God's Word being shared in a way that gives the Spirit opportunity to "prepare the soil" by challenging fundamental assumptions, commitments and alignments?
- Is Truth being shared with people in a way that leads them to stand honestly and humbly before God and to turn to Jesus Christ as God's answer to their deepest longings and needs?

? DISCUSSION POINTS

1. In your own words describe how you understand the relationship between the inherent power of God's Word and the role that teaching (i.e. sharing, explaining, discussing, preaching, etc.) plays in "activating" the power of God's Word.

2. Reflect on the idea that there are a variety of qualifications and gifts related to different Truth-sharing situations. Do you agree with this?

3. Imagine you start talking to someone on a plane. The flight will land in two hours and you're unlikely to ever see this person again. You sense they are searching and somewhat open but know very little about God's Word. In this hypothetical scenario you don't know how they'll respond, but in general, what will your approach be - what are the key things you would hope to ask, or to say?

7.8 The authority of God's Word

 OBJECTIVES OF THIS TUTORIAL

This tutorial discusses the third question in the area of *Word*: 'Are they learning to give God's Word its proper place and authority?'

Last time

In considering the whole range of situations in which Truth is being shared, we touched on the important aspect of language again. We also briefly talked about the inherent power of God's Word, and how that isn't brought into question in any way by us asking how we can best share and explain it in ways that unleash its power. Our mandate and authority to do this comes from Jesus Himself. But we do need to consider the attitudes, qualifications, gifting and equipping of those (ourselves included) who are sharing truth.

We also considered the hugely significant part that *worldview* plays and how those sharing Truth need to be committed to understanding their listeners' deeply held commitments and heart orientations...their *stories*. At some point the effective sharing of Truth challenges these things and leads people to stand before God empty handed and to turn to Jesus Christ as the only answer to their true needs.

The third question under "W" for *Word*

- Are they able to access the Bible in a form that clearly and faithfully communicates God's revelation to them?
- Are they having God's Word presented to them in a way that allows it to enter and engage their hearts at a worldview level?
- <u>Are they learning to give God's Word its proper place and authority?</u>
- Are they growing in their ability to correctly understand God's Word as His complete Narrative, with Jesus Christ as the heart of the story and its interpretive key?
- Are they increasingly able to make use of God's Word as He intends for His children and His Church?

For our immediate purposes we're defining the four areas of *Word*, *Identity*, *Life* and *Discipleship* separately, but in the reality of a situation they blend together in one "organic", seamless process. That's why the image of a Body is so apt when we're talking about the Church. Even though medical manuals might show separate schematics of the human nervous, digestive and circulatory systems, in a healthy human body all of those things function in unison. In the same way, even though we might define a particular area or ask a specific question about the life, growth and fruit of an individual, group or local church, to really understand these things we also have to see the connections between them.

We highlight that here because when we come to consider whether God's Word is being given its proper place and authority, it's not really an issue that can be considered in isolation. The questions we've already asked about the *form* and how well someone is actually understanding God's Word, and also about whether or not it is engaging them at a worldview level, are all very important factors that relate to the *authority* it is given. Likewise, the questions we'll be asking next under the area of *Word* impact, and are impacted by, this issue of authority.

God's authority not in question

But you might be wondering, "Why are we even asking about the authority of God's Word? Of course it has authority!" And yes, that's absolutely correct. But this is very similar to the issue we've already touched on about the *power* of His Word. Actually, as you'll no doubt already have noted, authority and power are very closely related. We said that the inherent power of God's Word is not in question, only whether we, as His co-workers, are allowing it the freedom to do what He intends. But, power and authority are also different: power can be impersonal, whereas authority is not. Authority implies that *someone has authority*, and also that *someone* is *under that authority* (whether they recognise it or not). So we know the truth of the first part of this equation; God's absolute, a-z, alpha to omega, beginning to end, authority - and that His authority, naturally, also applies to His Word.

So what we want to evaluate is whether people understand or acknowledge that they are under God's authority. In a situation where a person or group of people are hearing Truth shared, is it resulting in them putting themselves under the authority of that Truth, and the One who spoke it, the One who IS Truth? OR, are they maybe recognizing it as having *some* authority - *"Yes, it's important. Yes, it's right to listen to the Bible. Yes, I can see that I benefit from hearing what's shared. I want what this teaching offers... but on the whole it is only one of the "voices" I listen to. I might say, and even believe at some level, that it is the final authority, but does it actually shape my life? Is it changing the things I value...those worldview commitments and orientations of the heart?"*

Okay, what can we further identify about the kind of conversations, explanations, sharing, passing on, teaching or preaching of Truth that will see God's Word not be just *one* voice, but *the* Voice in the life of an individual or a group?

A cosmic battle

The outstanding, consistent characteristic of those who are sharing Truth effectively, is that they recognise the seriousness of the cosmic battle that is going on between Truth and lies. In the second of his letters to the Corinthians that we have recorded in the New Testament, Paul writes specifically about the preaching of the Good News which can be hidden, veiled, obscured by lies… and that's the reason, he says, people are perishing (2 Corinthians 4:3-4). A little later he says that when he and his co-workers are faithfully preaching Truth they are operating in God's power. They are using "weapons of righteousness" for both attack and defense (2 Corinthians 6:7). And further on, still in the language of warfare, he describes them using those mighty weapons of God "to knock down the strongholds of human reasoning and to destroy false arguments"… to "destroy every proud obstacle that keeps people from knowing God," and to "capture their rebellious thoughts and teach them to obey Christ" (2 Corinthians 10:4–5).

Writing to the Ephesian believers, Paul says they had better be well armed and well protected because they are in a fight that is light years beyond a physical, human level. It is against "…evil rulers and authorities of the unseen world, against mighty powers in this dark world, and against evil spirits in the heavenly places" (Ephesians 6:12). It's a life or death battle for the souls of human beings. And people are not just hanging around eager to submit to the authority of whatever we tell them, no matter how well intentioned or passionate we might be. There is another authority, Satan, who has usurped God's rule in this world, who has blinded their minds. He has effectively created a web of lies and an entire system of allegiances that are in direct opposition to God's authority.

When we share Truth with an individual or group still under Satan's control we are joining in the battle that is going on for control of their hearts and minds. We are contributing to God calling them "out of the darkness into his wonderful light" (1 Peter 2:9). This is a dramatic rescue effort in which God uses His Truth to break down the formidable defenses of the kingdom of darkness so He can rescue people and bring them under the loving reign of the Lord Jesus (Colossians 1:13). But even after that paradigm shift takes place and people are saved, it's not like the habits of those past allegiances disappear overnight; allegiances to self and to sinful desires, to a world system at odds with God's authority. It is the careful, intentional sharing of Truth that gradually washes away those lingering loyalties and allows God's people to live out of their true identity as His Temple, His Body, and His Bride (Ephesians 5:26,27).

In light of the sobering reality that every Truth-sharing opportunity represents a skirmish in this war being fought between Light and Darkness, we can ask these questions about those who are involved (including ourselves): Do they understand the life and death significance of what they are doing? Are they very consciously dependent on God for wisdom, grace and protection for themselves in the battle? Are they humbly putting themselves under the authority of God's Word and His Spirit and other authorities within the Body that God has provided for their guidance and encouragement? And are they taking every opportunity to equip themselves well for the battle?

There are no formulas

So that's about the <u>people</u> who are sharing Truth, but what about the <u>way</u> they share it? Of course there are no formulas. How people respond to Truth - whether or not they submit to God's rule as a result of what they hear - is part of the freedom that only a truly Sovereign God can give without compromising His absolute authority for a moment. He says that when He sends out His Word it always produces fruit and accomplishes what He intends (Isaiah 55:11). At the same time He talks about using us to appeal and plead with people to listen (2 Corinthians 5:20). But just because we have no control over how God chooses ultimately to use His Word on the one hand, or over our human audience's choices on the other, that doesn't mean we shouldn't have a plan. It shouldn't stop us from asking God to help us understand how to communicate in ways that reflect and establish the inherent authority of His Word.

There are many factors we could discuss at this point, and as we've said, the rest of the W.I.L.D. categories and questions will be relevant to this issue. But for now we'll touch very briefly on just two related characteristics of Truth-sharing that are vital if we're going to see people acknowledge God's rightful claims over them.

Addressing questions, meeting real needs

First, the Truth of God's Word should be communicated in such a way that it is seen to answer the big *existential* or *metaphysical* questions (e.g. How can we know anything to be true? Why do things exist? What is our purpose for being? Why is there evil and suffering? What happens after death? etc.). But the truth of God's Word should also be communicated so it is relevant to the normal experiences and struggles of life (e.g. How am I seen by others? What does it mean to be successful? Where do I turn to for comfort when I'm worried? How can I find security for myself and those I love? etc. In a non-Western, rural community the questions are likely to be about things like fertility and child birth, health, harvests, harmony in the community and protection from the spirits). One way these two areas have been contrasted is as *High Religion* and *Low* or *Folk Religion*. God's Word must be seen not only as authoritative in the areas people often equate with religion and "faith" but also in the reality of their everyday lives.

Secondly, Truth needs to be communicated so that it relates to people's <u>felt</u> needs in light of their <u>real</u> needs, i.e. as God defines them. As we get to know people and build relationships with them, it's often their felt needs that we relate about with them first. Listening to the things that concern them, the cries of their heart, their struggles and perhaps their achievements…this process forges important links between us and is often the only way we gain the right to share Truth with them. But as much as we might empathize and acknowledge their experiences, what they want, or how they'd like things to be better, it is not actually those things that should rule their lives. Satan's web of deceit places each person - temporarily and in his or her own mind - at the center of the universe ("You will be like God…" Genesis 3:5).

We're not saying that God's Word doesn't relate to people's felt needs. As we've said above, it has to be seen to be relevant to every question and area of our human experience. But God, the Creator, Father and Judge of the human race is the only One who can rightfully define how we stand before Him and therefore what our real needs are. Any time that God's Word is being discussed, taught or preached, the intention of His servants should be to help others hear Him clarify what it is they really need and how He alone has the right and ability to provide the answers. This puts felt needs in their correct perspective.

We've talked about the correct perspective those sharing Truth should have, and also a couple of things about how they can establish its authority; but what should we be looking for as evidence that, as our question puts it, an individual or group "are learning to give God's Word its proper place and authority?"

Changed lives

One of the first and most obvious things that we look for is changed lives. When Paul writes to the Colossians, he begins - as he often does in his letters - by telling them of the things about them that he regularly thanks God for. The Good News that was so effective when shared with them is also bearing fruit around the world, Paul says, in the form of changed lives (Colossians 1:5,6). This makes sense to us, doesn't it? We would expect that when a person or a group, perhaps a local church, is truly accepting the authority of God's Word in their lives, then they are going to change. They are going to align their values and therefore their behavior to God's true perspective that He is communicating through His Word and which is being explained to them through the teaching they are hearing.

The problem, of course, is that not all changes in behavior are the result of correct alignment with the Good News. There are endless examples of people who do certain things or stop doing others because they believe that will change the way God views them. That means they are not functioning according to Truth…in other words, a lie. And that, in turn, means that it is not actually His Word that they are submitting to, even though they might be hearing or reading the words of the Bible.

But if we look further at what Paul wrote to the Colossians, he says that this change in their lives he was so grateful for is the result of the hope that they now have and the understanding they have of God's grace. Similarly, when he writes to the Thessalonians and reflects on the powerful impact of the Good News, which he and others taught, he says that it brought them "full assurance" (1 Thessalonians 1:5–6). Their acceptance of the apostles' teaching had resulted in them going through "severe suffering" but that didn't take away the joy that the Gospel had given to them.

A confident, life-changing assurance about the central message of the Gospel, that Jesus has borne the full payment for their sin, goes against every fiber of someone's being… every instinct of their hearts and minds, every natural allegiance of the self, every worldview commitment. So when we see that assurance growing in someone, we know that they truly are submitting themselves to the authority of God's Word and that genuine alignment in their lives will be the result.

Some extra questions

To go along with the third question in the area of *Word*, 'Are they learning to give God's Word its proper place and authority?', we can now add some extra ones:

- Are those sharing Truth keenly aware of the battle, and is that causing them to humbly depend on God and to lean on others in the Body for encouragement, input and accountability?
- Is Truth being shared so that it's seen to answer the big questions of life, while also being relevant to everyday concerns; and are *felt* needs being addressed in light of people's *real* needs before God?
- Is the sharing of Truth resulting in a real understanding of God's grace, a joyful assurance of salvation, and changed lives?

❓ DISCUSSION POINTS

1. Oswald Chambers (1884 - 1917) said, *"There have been prophets and students who handle the Bible like a child's box of bricks; they explain to us the design and structure and purpose; but as time goes on things do not work out in their way at all. They have mistaken the scaffolding for the structure, while all the time God is working out His purpose with a great and undeterred patience."* What do you think he is saying about the area of "authority" here?

7.9 The complete Narrative

OBJECTIVES OF THIS TUTORIAL

This tutorial discusses the fourth question in the area of *Word*: 'Are they growing in their ability to correctly understand God's Word as His complete Narrative, with Jesus Christ as the heart of the story and its interpretive key?'

Last time

We noted that, although we're defining specific things in different categories in the life of a healthy, growing individual or group, those things actually function together seamlessly. As far as effectively establishing the authority of God's Word, there are many factors that work together. We stressed that its inherent authority is not in question; what we're wanting to understand is how that authority is *established* and what we should see when it is.

We noted these three points about the authority of God's Word being established:

- It is established by those who take the battle seriously, who know how to protect themselves, and how to use Truth effectively for breaking down the Enemy's defenses.
- It is shared in such a way that it is seen to answer both the big and small questions of life, and it addresses felt needs in light of real needs, i.e. real as God defines them.
- It is evidenced by people coming to a real understanding of God's grace, having a joyful assurance of salvation and through changed lives.

The fourth question under "W" for *Word*

- Are they able to access the Bible in a form that clearly and faithfully communicates God's revelation to them?
- Are they having God's Word presented to them in a way that allows it to enter and engage their hearts at a worldview level?
- Are they learning to give God's Word its proper place and authority?
- <u>Are they growing in their ability to correctly understand God's Word as His complete Narrative, with Jesus Christ as the heart of the story and its interpretive key?</u>
- Are they increasingly able to make use of God's Word as He intends for His children and His Church?

This topic is another example of what we've already stressed: even though it is helpful for us to define these different threads of God's work in people's lives, these things don't function in isolation from each other. In the previous tutorial (7.8) we were talking about how the *authority* of God's Word is established. Now we're going to focus on how a correct *understanding* of God's Word comes about through seeing it as one complete and cohesive Narrative. But we should also notice the implications for authority here as well.

We've said previously that the actual authority of God is realized when His voice - His Word - is what dominates and shapes our thinking; when our ideas and experience are interpreted according to what He says. That authority breaks down (not in reality, but in how we submit to it) when there are gaps and inconsistencies. Of course sometimes this is the result of straightforward rebellion - when we know something to be true and yet we refuse to listen. But often our failures to yield to His authority are the result of confusion and not understanding how to relate Truth consistently to some area of life.

Let's imagine two hypothetical examples from very different settings:

1. Chris and Emma...

...who are both from non-believing backgrounds, have been living together for the last year. They hear the Gospel through a webcast and are saved. They start to occasionally attend a home group where they meet some couples who are married, unlike all their other friends. They also begin to have some questions about how to relate to some friends who are gay. In the past they had assumed, just like everyone else they knew, that homosexuality is a life-style choice and that anyone opposed to it is just intolerant and stuck in the past. Now they're not so sure, but they don't want to just unthinkingly assume a "Christian" perspective. They would really like to know what God says about all of this, but where do they start?

2. Mulu...

...a teenager, has been a believer for two years. His daily work is helping in the communal rice fields and vegetable gardens that provide food and also cash from the traders who come up from the coast in trucks each month. Twice a year the village gets together to sacrifice pigs to enlist the help of the spirits in ensuring good crops. Mulu has heard from some Christians in town that God does not want His children to be involved in such things. Normally he just keeps in the background at the sacrifice and the last couple of times he's managed to quietly avoid eating the pig meat. But this time he has been chosen to represent his clan in the actual ritual sacrifice. To refuse will bring shame on his family. Everyone will believe that he's putting the spiritual harmony, and their livelihood in jeopardy. Surely God won't mind? What is he to do? How can he know what God's Word says?

Are more Bible verses the solution?

A natural assumption we can make in thinking about these situations is that the missing ingredient is information; more Bible references - that what Chris and Emma and Mulu need most in their respective dilemmas is to be pointed to some Bible verses, perhaps with some teaching to help explain them. And indeed this may be helpful. Certainly seeing what God's Word says about some related circumstances or hearing specific instructions and exhortations that have been given in the past is not in itself a bad thing. But here are some questions worth asking:

- Do they have a sufficient framework of understanding about the character of God for this section of the Bible to fit into?
- Do they have enough background to place this portion of God's Word at least somewhat in its context? (Who was God communicating to and for what purpose? How is God's character and His purpose being revealed?)
- Do they have an accurate picture of the Bible overall, especially in terms of its relevance to their daily lives?
- Do they see these passages as integral parts of God's one, seamless Truth (i.e. rather than as scraps of Christian teaching...possibly true, but in a weak, fragmented sense)?
- If they try to apply what they're hearing to their own circumstances will it be based on a clear understanding of God's actual view of them (i.e. rather than because they are trying to be worthy and to build credit with Him)?

Even though their cultural landscapes look very different, the formative worldviews of Chris and Emma and also Mulu are *pluralistic* - they are worldviews where Satan has successfully eroded the idea of absolutes. In a modern - or "post-modern" - humanist society, believing in one universal Truth (and any applications of it) is despised as outdated, intolerant fundamentalism. In turn, animistic worldviews are notoriously adept at absorbing new belief systems and holding them simultaneously, even if they appear contradictory to an outsider.

So with those backgrounds, how then can they come to see God's Word as completely authoritative? How can they have their dilemmas addressed in such a way that they will be entirely confident that this is God's voice and not just the opinion of some Christians or a church? And if they are exposed to a portion of God's Word that seems to address the issue at hand, how can they know they're interpreting it correctly? What will protect them from the "Scripture-twisting" and confusion of the many cults and sects that would gladly draw them in? What would it take, if we were trying to disciple them, to answer the five questions above in the positive? (Try going back and reading those questions again as statements: "They have…" "They see…" "When they try…" etc.)

Before going on, let's remind ourselves of the original W.I.L.D. question that we're considering: *Are they growing in their ability to correctly understand God's Word as His complete Narrative, with Jesus Christ as the heart of the story and its interpretive key*?

What if Narrative foundations had been laid?

Chris and Emma and Mulu have some immediate concerns, and if you had the opportunity to be part of their journey of faith, you would obviously need to give them some timely encouragement and help. But think how well prepared they'd be for anything you'd share with them if they'd already been exposed to God's Word as His complete Narrative. What if they had a clear understanding of how and why God created the universe, the world and ultimately, human beings? Imagine if you had been able to stand alongside them, as it were, and comment while together you'd observed God's earliest interactions with this race of His image-bearers that He'd made. If you'd watched with them when they heard about how Adam and Eve listened to Satan and then saw God's interaction with them and His response. And what if you'd been able to keep walking with them, so to speak, down through history, experiencing the highlights of God's record of His engagement with human beings? Until eventually you'd been able to introduce them to the promised Messiah, the Rescuer…and beside His disciples walked the roads of Palestine, and sat on a hillside while He healed people and shared God's message with them. And most importantly, if you'd helped them see how all the threads of who God is, and what He's shown us about Himself, come together in His Son, and are demonstrated most clearly in His death, burial and resurrection.

Even if you've not had that personal privilege, and someone else has been their "guide" for those initial stages, what a great foundation and reservoir of Truth you're now working with as you try to help and encourage them! They might be very new believers, but if their path to faith has involved getting to know God, themselves, Satan and eventually Jesus the Saviour through God's Narrative, then there will be many important areas of Truth you'll be able to confidently work from. Here are just a few general areas:

- In coming to know God as the sovereign, communicating Creator, the underlying pluralism in their respective worldviews has been seriously challenged and is being replaced with new worldview commitments and certainties.
- They've seen God always, without exception or contradiction, relate to everyone on the basis of His absolute righteousness and love.
- They know that God has specific purposes for human beings and that down through history He has revealed those purposes in His Word.
- In numerous and varied ways they've had God's Narrative challenge the deeply ingrained human assumption that they can *do* something to appease or please Him through their own efforts.

Specific foundations for Chris and Emma

How about some specific areas of Truth you would be able to remind Chris and Emma about as they wrestle with issues of morality for themselves and their friends? From their initial introduction to God's Narrative they already know that:

- Having designed and created the first man, God then perfectly fulfilled Adam's need for close human companionship through the woman He created.
- Adam and Eve's special marriage relationship was vitally tied into God's purpose for his image-bearing race. Together, as man and wife, they were to relate to Him while overseeing His creation and populating the earth with other human God-worshippers.
- The capture and Fall of the human race by Satan's deceit was integrally tied into their failure as a husband/wife couple to humbly seek God's guidance. All human relationships, and most importantly the marriage and family ones, have ever since been confused, and much of the tragedy facing the human race can be traced to this.
- It's clear from God's Law that His standards for morality are absolute and therefore impossible for humans in their own strength to fulfill.
- Jesus Christ is the only One who has fulfilled God's perfect Law in every dimension and related to God the Father in the way He intends for humans.

- Having put their faith in Jesus, Chris and Emma's relationship with God has been restored. They now have a wonderful opportunity to align their lives with the purpose that God originally intended for Adam and Eve.
- Their friends, 'straight' or 'gay', just like everyone else who's not saved, are under God's judgment and equally in desperate need of Him to save them.

Specific foundations for Mulu

What if it was Mulu who'd come to you for help in his difficult dilemma with the sacrifices? If, in the process of coming to know Jesus Christ as His Saviour, he also had the chance to hear the broad sweep of God's Narrative, what specific foundations of Truth would now be accessible to him? He already knows that:

- Satan has skillfully deceived all human groups and communities under his dominion to keep them from knowing and believing God.
- One of Satan's favorite strategies is to encourage people to trust in and worship some replacement for the true God.
- God's perfect Law demands that humans must always, under every circumstance, worship God with every part of their being.
- Only Jesus Christ has proved able to give God the place that He deserves.
- When Mulu put his faith in Jesus he was taken by God out of Satan's control and placed in God's family. This position of safety is permanent because it has nothing to do with Mulu's own actions; it is entirely dependent on the righteousness of Jesus.
- This does not mean that Mulu will face no problems in this world. Beginning with Cain, many people who are trusting in something other than God's provision have been used by Satan to oppose God's people.
- Jesus showed love to His own community but He would not bow to pressure to be involved in things He knew would detract from God's message. He was persecuted for His stance.
- Jesus has given us His Spirit and has promised that He will be with us at all times no matter what difficulties we face as His people in this world.

Even though for the purpose of this illustration, Chris and Emma and Mulu are so far only familiar with the highlights from the Old Testament and the Gospels, this amount of Truth has already provided a great basis for them to see the Bible as one body of Truth that is totally relevant to their current circumstances. The things God has revealed about Himself, about them and all humans, about Satan and then about the Lord Jesus Christ, give them a solid basis for knowing God's perspective about their current circumstances and dilemmas. They do not have to wonder if they are misunderstanding a particular fragment of the Bible or whether it is being presented from some prejudiced perspective. The Truth they can apply here and now is built solidly on what God has shown them clearly through His Narrative. Of course He wants to continue to build on those foundations of Truth already in place and see them mature further as His children, and this will happen best if they continue to engage with God's Word in the same way rather than engaging with fragments that are extracted from their real-life Narrative context.

This topic of how people can confidently interpret and apply the Bible to their lives deserves a lot more consideration than we've been able to give it in this one tutorial. But before we finish, let's briefly note two more things.

Christ as interpretive key

The W.I.L.D. question in focus talks about Jesus Christ being the "interpretive key" through whom we arrive at correct understandings of God's Word. There is a wealth of writing about this topic that can help us gain further insights into Jesus Christ's central place in interpretation or *hermeneutics* and we'd do well to access some of what's written by reliable writers. Although we've not had the space here to even begin exploring that area specifically, it's worth nothing that this did emerge as we were picturing the truth-foundations that we'd be able to draw from if Chris and Emma and Mulu had engaged with Truth initially as one complete Christ-focused Narrative. As the central figure of history and as the One who is at the heart of the Narrative - He makes sense of it all.

Interpreting God's Narrative as a group

The second point is this: as we've briefly delved into this fourth W.I.L.D. question, we've focused on individuals learning to interpret and apply God's Word as He intends. Although it is obviously important for each person to be equipped to correctly interpret what they hear, read and experience, the reality is that God does not intend for His children to engage with His Word as isolated individuals. To re-visit our scenarios one last time: imagine how much better it would be for Chris and Emma if they were wrestling with their different moral questions with other believers who were also being equipped to apply God's Narrative Truth consistently in their lives. Or how much encouragement Mulu would get in facing the disapproval and possible rejection of his village if he was part of a group who shared the same Truth foundations and relationship with Jesus Christ as he does.

Some extra questions

To go along with the fourth question under *Word*, 'Are they growing in their ability to correctly understand God's Word as His complete Narrative, with Jesus Christ as the heart of the story and its interpretive key?', we can also ask:

- Has their initial engagement with Truth introduced them to God as Creator and Lord, to Satan as Enemy, to humanity as God's completely lost race of image-bearers, and to Jesus Christ as Saviour?
- Do they understand the Biblical Narrative as God's revelation to real people, living in real times and places, and are new areas of truth being tied in historically and thematically with what they've already understood?
- Are they being integrated into a group of disciples where they are being helped to interpret and apply God's Word appropriately to their everyday experiences?

? DISCUSSION POINTS

1. Can you think of an example from your own experience that illustrates someone - either yourself or someone else - facing one of the big questions or dilemmas in life and applying God's Word to it in order to find understanding or comfort?

2. What do you think is the cultural foundation (the culture of the people in the world around you) for solving the big questions or dilemmas that life brings? Do people typically apply logic, are they mystical, do they search for answers in a cohesive overarching story or are they happy to accommodate mutually contradictory concepts?

3. How does a cohesive view of the Biblical Narrative illustrate a person's understanding of God's character?

7.10 Making use of God's Word

✓ OBJECTIVES OF THIS TUTORIAL

This tutorial discusses the fifth question in the area of *Word*: 'Are they increasingly able to make use of God's Word as He intends for His children and His Church?'

Last time

We explored the idea that a cohesive understanding of God's Word (or Narrative) establishes its authority. To consider how this works in reality we imagined two scenarios of new believers from very different contexts who are wrestling with dilemmas. We then considered five questions that might help us decide whether sharing a specific passage from the Bible would be most helpful for them. Also, given that they come from pluralistic worldview foundations, we noted the importance of them having rock-solid foundations of Truth to trust and to live by. We then imagined the advantages if their initial engagement with God's Word had introduced Him and Jesus Christ to them through the Narrative.

The fifth question under "W" for *Word*

- Are they able to access the Bible in a form that clearly and faithfully communicates God's revelation to them?

- Are they having God's Word presented to them in a way that allows it to enter and engage their hearts at a worldview level?

- Are they learning to give God's Word its proper place and authority?

- Are they growing in their ability to correctly understand God's Word as His complete Narrative, with Jesus Christ as the heart of the story and its interpretive key?

- <u>Are they increasingly able to make use of God's Word as He intends for His children and His Church?</u>

There's a fairly obvious sequence that you'll have noticed in these initial five questions. In effect, we've been following the steps of how God's Truth - when it's communicated clearly and effectively - first establishes its own authority, then cultivates faith, develops correct understanding and leads to valid applications. Finally, in this last one, we're considering how the Word equips God's people to *use* it productively. Having understood, believed, submitted and begun to relate it more widely to their lives, now they begin to learn how to ably use it as God's servants.

But there's also another related progression we should remind ourselves of. As we said earlier in the module, in presenting this W.I.L.D. framework, we've avoided calling it a "church planting model" or even "church growth model". That's because we don't want to infer that it's only about situations where a number of people are involved from the outset. In many contexts a church starts with an individual being saved, then another, and so on. So we wanted to consider how Truth impacts people, whether an individual, a couple, a family, or indeed a much bigger group.

A community of His people

The reality is that we can't really evaluate the ongoing impact of God's Word without fairly quickly bringing the Church - His Body - into the equation. While Truth can be shared by just one isolated believer with another individual, that's not ultimately God's intention, either for the one sharing or the one being impacted. And that's where we can see another inbuilt progression in these questions (i.e. these first five, but also as we move into the other areas of W.I.L.D.).

We might possibly say that the first and second questions could be applied to a one-on-one scenario; *Are they able to access the Bible in a form that clearly and faithfully communicates God's revelation to them? Are they having God's Word presented to them in a way that allows it to enter and engage their hearts at a worldview level*? But when we come to the third question - *Are they learning to give God's Word its proper place and authority?* - and really delve into how the authority of God's Word is established, it quickly becomes obvious that it doesn't happen in a relational vacuum. We know that God has created us, like Himself, as distinct individuals; but it's also true that like the Trinity - the three-in-one Unity of God - He relates to us as individuals-in-a-community. And in this time of history, that community in which He relates to His people is, of course, the *Ecclesia*, the Church. So again, in terms of how authority is established, yes, it's within an individual's heart as they stand before God, but it's also as they willingly submit to God's Spirit speaking to them through other brothers and sisters; hearing, experiencing and living it out together.

And then again with the fourth question - *Are they growing in their ability to correctly understand God's Word as His complete Narrative, with Jesus Christ as the heart of the story and its interpretive key?* - as we've already touched on, arriving at correct understanding of what God's Word means and how to apply it is not a theoretical process one believer is meant to do in isolation. Even though there are many examples of God speaking to individuals - Abraham, Noah, Moses, David, Paul, John, etc. - it was always with the intention of them sharing that message to a community of His people. The role of His designated prophets and apostles was not only to speak His Word, but also to draw out its meaning and practical implications for the community of faith.

Now, as we ask this fifth question about whether those hearing Truth are growing in their ability to make use of God's Word, it's really not possible to consider that outside the context of a body of believers. That conviction is reflected in the wording of the question itself which talks about God's intentions *for His children and His Church*. So our first five questions that started out considering quite abstract concepts have now come down to some very tangible, practical issues - how people are actually *using* God's Word. And again, that use, if it's valid, if it's what Christ intends, will be in and through the lives of believers who are learning to function as part of the corporate life of His Body.

Hopefully it's clear by now that when we employ a term like *making use of God's Word* we're not meaning to treat it just as information, a piece of equipment, or as some kind of commodity. We don't have to look further than the Psalms to find many very emotional and passionate examples of how we are meant to see the Scriptures. At the same time, God's Word describes itself as functioning like a fire and a tool (Jeremiah 23:29), a lamp and a light (Psalm 119:105), protective armor and weaponry (Hebrews 4:12, Ephesians 6:11-17), as a catalyst for change (2 Timothy 3:16) and the material with which His servants work.

But how *do* we use God's Word appropriately? What reference points should we utilize to gauge whether or not those hearing Truth are learning to make use of it? Obviously there are many ways we could sort and describe these, but maybe three concepts borrowed from agriculture will be apt: *nurture*, *shape* and *propagate*.

Nurture (to care for and protect)

Someone who is learning to make use of God's Word is able to feed themselves. If they are accessing Truth at a worldview level, if its authority has been established in their lives if and they're learning to make sense of each new part in light of the whole, then they are in a position of being able to find nourishment from the Word.

Certainly God makes it very clear that He gives specific abilities and responsibilities within the Ecclesia for the feeding of His *children*, His *flock*. But just as clear is His intention for believers to be motivated and equipped to feed themselves from His Word. At the risk of badly mixing our metaphors, remember how the apostle Peter used the image of a baby craving milk (1 Peter 2:2). There's a clear implication that a child craves the food that's appropriate to what it can digest at a particular stage of its development. Growth toward maturity is a process that starts with someone completely dependent on others for nourishment gradually progressing to a point where they're able to feed themselves - without, of course, negating the critical role of God's Spirit and fellow believers all along the way.

Paul puts the responsibility on the Colossians (Colossians 1:23) to continue to believe the Good News they've been taught and to "stand firmly" in it. To let their "roots grow down into Him (Christ)" and that their "lives be built on Him" (Colossians 2:7). So the nurture of new believers is most definitely the responsibility of any who share God's Word and those who are placed in positions of leadership within the Body. But as we evaluate a given situation in which Truth is being shared, a clear sign of maturity is when individuals within the Body are also learning to *use* God's Word for their own nourishment and growth.

But most plants or trees don't grow in a laboratory, or even a greenhouse. They're trying to make it out in the real world where they're vulnerable to the extremes of weather and attacks from disease and pests. Of course a healthy plant is also one that can handle heat, cold, insect infestation, mold etc. (We're reminded here of Jesus' parable of the sower and the importance of careful planting.) But even healthy plants often need some strategy to protect them from devastating environmental conditions and pathogens. Careful farmers are aware of what is most likely to harm their crops and take measures to guard against that.

The applications to those growing in their faith are obvious. But maybe the agricultural analogy runs out, because God's intention for His children is not for them to remain in a vulnerable state of relying on others for protection. There is, without doubt, protection to be found within a body of believers (that's why church discipline is designed to be so devastating to an unrepentant Christian). But God also wants each believer to come to a point of maturity where they can *use* His Word, not only to feed themselves but also to protect against attack.

To illustrate this in his letter to the Ephesians, Paul uses two images from activities that would have been familiar to the church in Ephesus. The first, (Ephesians 4:14), pictures immature believers as small rudderless boats on a stormy ocean, being helplessly pushed around by every gust of wind that comes their way. Paul says in preceding verses that God has given His Word through the apostles and prophets, and also gifted His servants to teach that Word, specifically to help believers move beyond that vulnerable, immature state. They are to be *equipped* with a rudder and the ability to steer a course - in other words, to be able to instinctively apply Truth to the values of the society, in conversations, within relationships, in moments of emotional vulnerability, in the face of temptation. The supreme example we have of this is, of course, the way Jesus used Scripture to combat Satan's insidious attack on the Father-Son relationship that God had just attested to after Jesus' baptism.

Another striking image Paul uses in the epistle to the Ephesians is to describe believers as defending themselves in warfare (Ephesians 6:10-17). The armor and weapons they're to use, to a large degree, are made available to them through the efforts of God's servants who share Truth in the Body. But each believer is exhorted to put the armor on, to pick up the shield, to know how to wield the sword. No one can hope to stay safe for too long if they always have to hide behind someone else's shield and sword and never join the battle themselves.

Shape (to train and prune)

Most fruit bearing vines, bushes and trees are healthiest and most productive when they are shaped in specific ways: by being trained onto a frame or trellis, through pruning, or a combination of the two. Opening them up to light and air encourages fruit and reduces the chance of disease and insect attack. In His famous description of Himself as the true vine and His people as the branches, Jesus says, "You have already been pruned and purified by the message I have given you." (John 15:3). God's revelation of His Truth is the way in which He shapes His people for the lives and work He designed them for.

But we're not talking about topiary - you know, when shrubs are trimmed into weird, tortured shapes like spirals or animals. And it's not bonsai - keeping plants unnaturally dwarfed by restricting the growth of their roots and branches. Jesus said that knowing the truth would set His followers *free* (John 8:31–32). When we see the Bible being used by believers to place themselves or others under Law, to generate fear, or to coerce people to live up to human expectations, we can readily identify that as an improper use of His Word. The kind of training and pruning we are talking about is based on the amazing reality that believers have been freed from the Law through their participation in Jesus' death and resurrection. That's why; Paul explains to the believers in Rome (Romans 7:4-5), they are now able to "produce a harvest of good deeds for God".

Of course humans have been deceived into believing that real freedom is all about doing whatever their appetites and inclinations dictate. Ironically, as God's Word makes clear, that is actually the ultimate slavery. Through Christ He has made His children free, not to be slaves to their own sin-corrupted wills, but to do *His* will, to do what He created them for. This new freedom involves learning a whole new set of habits and behaviors. Thankfully, He has given His Word, *breathed* out from His own holy, powerful being, to reveal what needs to be changed, to correct what is wrong and give us the opportunity to do things that God delights in (2 Timothy 3:16).

When Paul, under the Spirit's guidance, was reflecting on Scripture that way, it was in the context of encouraging Timothy in his ministry among the believers in Ephesus. He chose a term, which in modern English is often translated as "useful". He was telling his young friend to view God's Word as something that has very real, practical benefits. It works! It's not just theoretical truth, not just religious dogma, certainly not a set of confining rules. God's Word is a wonderful resource, a functioning toolbox that was available to Timothy and all believers; to parents, disciplers, teachers and church leaders. Or to go back to our agricultural analogy, it is the trellis God provides to give us the shape that we're meant to be, the pruning shears that in His loving hands leave only what's healthy and productive.

Propagate (to spread and reproduce)

A third area to consider in how individuals or groups of believers are *using* God's Word, is how well they are learning to pass Truth on to others. Genesis records that when God first created the vegetation that covers the planet, He said that each species would reproduce the same kind of plants and trees. This wasn't a fatherly, divine suggestion; it was a sovereign command. Plants *will* produce seed, they *will* be fruitful, they *will* spread out, and they *will* reproduce. It is a force built into their DNA by their Creator. If you've ever been in a tropical, rainforest area, you'll have a sense of just how powerfully this drive to propagate can be in certain ecosystems - the verdant riot of growing things everywhere can be almost overwhelming.

Isaiah likens the rain God sends to water food crops, with Him sending out His Word to feed people spiritually. In words that echo His proclamation about the fruitfulness of trees and plants at Creation, God says that His Word always produces fruit. It accomplishes everything He wants it to (Isaiah 55:10-11).

But as the apostle Paul reminds the believers in Rome, God has determined that in the normal course of events, if lost people are going to hear the Good News, it will be through His people taking it to them. But they need to be sent, to know they are sent (Romans 10:14-15). And that is a beautiful thing…God's people intentionally going out to share Truth - ordinary, weak, very human people, but with a wonderful treasure to share (2 Corinthians 4:7). This spreading out, this self-seeding, is something built into the DNA of the Church in the same way that God built fruitfulness into the plants and trees of creation. So yes, we would hope to see groups of believers like a garden or orchard that is nurtured and watered, well protected from disease and infestation and also enjoying the freedom that comes with being shaped and pruned by God's Word.

But a healthy tree sets fruit. It seeds and reproduces itself. In the same way, when God's Word is doing what He intends for it to do among His people, we can expect to see people who know they are sent… a group who knows how to reach out. We should see them sharing God's Word clearly and faithfully so that it is understood; presenting Truth so it engages with people's hearts at a worldview level; teaching so that God's Word is given its proper place and authority; sharing in such a way that people understand God's complete Narrative with Jesus Christ as its center.

Some extra questions

To go along with the fifth question under *Word*, 'Are they increasingly able to make use of God's Word as He intends for His children and His Church?', we can also ask:

- Are they learning to use God's Word to spiritually feed themselves and to defend against attacks from the Enemy?
- Are they using Truth practically to correct wrong thinking and habits of life, not in a way that produces fear and bondage, but real joy and freedom in Christ?
- Are they learning to reach out with the Good News of Jesus Christ so it is communicated clearly and faithfully within the Biblical Narrative?

MAKING USE OF GOD'S WORD

❓ DISCUSSION POINTS

1. Imagine you move to a new town and become part of a small house church. Finding out that you have thought and studied about how churches grow to maturity, they invite you to evaluate the impact of God's Word on their group. How do you think you'd go about this? Where would you start? What situations would you want to be in to make observations?

2. If you care to, please share anything you've been learning about making use of God's Word in any of the three ways highlighted here: nurture, shaping and propagation.

7.11 Understanding true identity

 OBJECTIVES OF THIS TUTORIAL

This tutorial introduces the area of *Identity*, and discusses the first question in that area: 'Are they increasingly clear about - and able to articulate - their true identity from God's perspective?'

Last time

We reminded ourselves that although, obviously, it is possible for an isolated individual or handful of people to be saved and even to begin to grow spiritually, real maturity is meant to happen within an *ecclesia*, a local church body. Learning to make *use* of God's Word as He intends (the focus of the fifth W.I.L.D. question) is something that only really happens within a supportive community of believers.

Using an agricultural metaphor, we defined three areas of practical use that God has given His Word for: *Nurture* - the spiritual food and protection that believers need in their daily lives. *Shape* - the discipline and correction from God's Word that produces holiness and freedom in Christ. *Propagate* - the motivation and ability to reach out faithfully with God's Message to others.

Identity

Now we want to go on to consider the second of the four W.I.L.D. lenses that we're using to observe situations where Truth is being shared. Of the four, *Identity* often seems to be the one that is most challenging to really understand. That may be because it's a fairly abstract concept. The dictionary defines *Identity* as "the fact of being who or what a person or thing is"; and to help clarify, it adds, "the characteristics determining who or what a person or thing is". Hmmm, well that clears it up, doesn't it?

Of course in the everyday world we use things like names, photographs, birth certificates, driver's licenses and credit cards to establish identity. But that doesn't go very far in helping us understand *who* someone really is. We can find out a lot more if we get a chance to hear their story.

UNDERSTANDING TRUE IDENTITY

It happens regularly on aeroplanes, doesn't it? During the course of the flight, total strangers sitting next to each other share a lot of their identities with each other - or at least what they want to project. Often their stories come out in bits and pieces…where they're going, where they're from, what they do for work, if they're married or not. They don't usually start out by saying, "Hey, can I share my identity? Let me tell you who I am." But if they keep talking, you usually find out a lot about the way they view themselves.

And on a more casual level, it's a process going on all the time. We see someone on the street and based on their facial features, the way they dress, their hairstyle, who they're with, their accent…and numerous other subtle things, we 'place' them; we figure out some things about their identity. We're not naturally objective about this. Usually without realizing, our cultural norms and personal preferences create the categories we use for establishing identity: this person's status, their place in society, how we view them and how we feel we should relate to them.

Using those same, mostly subconscious categories, we also try to project something about ourselves. What we wear is often not just a practical decision; we are conveying something to others about how we see ourselves and how we want to be seen. And this often changes depending on the setting - our clothes, yes, but also the message we're sending. The way we present ourselves, and therefore the identity we assume, is influenced by the identity and opinions of those we're with. Because we don't exist in a vacuum, identity is a kind of synthesis of the way we see ourselves and the way others see us. *Who am I in my family? Among my peers? In my church?*

Group identity

These principles relating to identity are true for groups as well as for individuals. Groups have internal definitions for themselves, but then they are also defined by external categorizations. So although a group's sense of identity is shaped by its past, it is also constantly being reshaped by the present. For example, the way a minority ethnic group is seen by a larger, dominant group, impacts their own sense of identity. If they are valued because their presence somehow benefits the community, then the ways they identify themselves will reflect a positive, secure sense of being. If, on the other hand, they are despised and mistrusted as a group, they might react by strengthening and hiding *behind* their ethnic identity as though under siege, or by trying to assimilate and escape the evidence of their ethnicity.

That leads to another observation. For a group to even exist as a group means defining not only who they *are* but also who they *are not*. Who is "us" and who is "them"? And that gets to the very significant issue of boundaries. How a group defines who's in and who's not, says a lot about what kind of group they are - in reality as well as how they and others perceive them.

Some groups are very casual: for example, *people traveling in Istanbul on Tuesday*. Others are more definite but ad hoc: for example, *passengers on the Turkish Airlines Tuesday morning flight from Istanbul to Moscow*. Some are much more formally defined: *the aircrew on that Turkish Airlines flight*. Others are quite definite, but more relationally fixed: *the family sitting in row 38*. Others are bounded by mutual interests: *members of a music lovers club from London on their way to Moscow for a concert at the Bolshoi Theatre*.

Obviously we could spend a lot of time on this, but here are a few tentative observations:

- There many different kinds - almost an infinite variety - of groups.
- We can "belong" to many different overlapping groups.
- Purpose often has something to do with group identity.
- There are many ways of defining the "in-or-out" boundaries of a group.
- How those boundaries are defined impacts and reflects on the way individuals view their membership in the group.

We'll talk a lot more about groups and make some specific applications in upcoming tutorials. Hopefully, even in this brief introduction, we're seeing that the issue of identity is a complex one. But it's also extremely important - not least of all to us as we're trying to evaluate how effectively Truth is being shared in a given situation.

Taking on His identity

One day in a hilly area at the head of the Jordan river valley, Jesus prompted His disciples to consider this topic of identity in light of how well people were understanding the Truth He'd been sharing (Matthew 16:13-16). But He didn't ask about people's sense of their own identity. He wanted to put the spotlight on something much more foundational: who the people understood that *He* was. And then, of course, He went on to ask the disciples who *they* understood Him to be. Peter's answer demonstrated that the substrate of Truth was firmly in place for him by correctly identifying Jesus as the Messiah, the Son of the Living God. This truth, Jesus said, was the foundation on which He'd build His Church.

Another time, when Philip asked Jesus to show them the Father (John 14:8-11), Jesus questioned how much His disciple has understood from being with Him. He should know by now that Jesus and God the Father are one. They are one in essential being, one in identity. Jesus said that this understanding comes by faith and through observing Him in action…seeing that everything He does is just as the Father would do it.

Years later, in a letter to the believers in Philippi, the apostle Paul shared how coming to know Jesus had radically impacted his view of himself (Philippians 3:5-9). His words portray a strong sense of how proud he'd formerly been of his identity - impeccable religious credentials, first-class education, ethnically pure, faultless family background - but when Jesus identified Himself so dramatically to the young Pharisee now lying on the road, he'd suddenly seen himself in a completely different light. All the previous tags and labels he'd been so proud of were shown up as pathetic and worthless. Everything had been totally eclipsed by the opportunity to share an identity with Jesus and to be covered by His righteousness before God.

Someone responding in faith to Truth that's shared effectively with them will come to a correct understanding of who God is and who Jesus Christ is. And that understanding is the only correct basis from which a human being can understand who they are. As we've thought about before, humans are taken up with themselves and telling their own stories, of reaffirming to themselves and others that they are someone of value. But what they really need is to stop thinking and talking about themselves and to listen to God tell His Story, to hear Him as Creator and Father describe Himself. Intertwined in His Narrative, of course, is the true account of who He made humans to be. Created in His image for specific purposes, tasked with being caretakers of His Creation (as we briefly noted above, *identity* and *purpose* are very closely related concepts). But then the Fall… and the identity fundamentally shifts. Now Adam's offspring are broken, excluded, followers of God's Enemy, rebellious, guilty. And yet, because of His grace, the human race is still loved by God, the ones He seeks after, the ones He promises to save.

At some point then, individuals need to find themselves standing before God's throne, with all their sense of self, their pride in who they are, everything society and Satan tells them they are…with all of that stripped away. Now seeing themselves as He sees them, who they actually are; sinful, needy, hopeless, guilty, but still loved. Then to find themselves standing at the foot of the Cross, seeing the One who is worthy in their place, having taken on Himself *their* identity as the condemned. Later, before the empty tomb, with all the wonderful implications: now they are the risen, the forgiven, the redeemed, a new creation, and children of God.

The first question under "*I*" for *Identity*

- Are they increasingly clear about - and able to articulate - their true identity from God's perspective?
- Are they learning to see their story embedded in the larger Narrative of the Church, stretching back to Pentecost and forward to Christ's return?
- Are they growing in their understanding of the bonds that unite them to the global/local Body under Christ as its Head?
- Are they learning to view others according to truth, and rejecting the divisions, biases and tensions that often define the wider society?
- Are they growing in their understanding of how to appropriately represent the Lord in their current spheres of contact and in others He might lead them to be involved in?

Obviously we can't expect every believer - young or old - to be able to give an exhaustive, theological treatise on his or her identity. But questions that touch on the topic and give someone an opportunity to reflect on how God sees them, are well worth including in a conversation. We might ask them to reflect on how they once saw themselves, before they came to know the Lord, in contrast to how they see themselves now. We might be able to ask directly how they believe God sees them now, and why. And at some point we would be echoing Jesus' question to His disciples and ask them who they understand that He is.

So what kind of responses would encourage us that their engagement with Truth is proving to be effective? We would hear them, first of all, focusing more on God than themselves. Anything they say that highlights Him, His majesty, righteousness and grace would obviously demonstrate a foundational understanding. And of course their thoughts and words would move naturally to speak of Jesus Christ, as their Lord and Saviour. It would be reassuring to hear them reflect on how their former perspective had changed, how they'd come to see themselves as lost and hopeless before God. And we'd be excited if they expressed a conviction that now, because of Jesus' sacrifice on their behalf, they are forgiven, cleansed, righteous in God's eyes.

And conversely, it would be very troubling to find that someone who has been exposed to the Bible was still talking mostly about themselves, still trying to affirm their value as a person, and giving indications that they see themselves as inherently worthy before God.

If you have been through the Biblical Foundations part of the *AccessTruth Curriculum*, you'll remember that in Module 2, before moving further into the Acts account of the early Church, we took some time to review what we had already covered from God's Narrative in Module 1. The difference, you'll recall, is that in Module 2 we looked back through the lens of all that Jesus has accomplished on our behalf. We celebrated the new identity that every believer has in Christ.

When we celebrate this new identity though, we also remember that we're not alone in this new life and identity. As we stand *in Christ*, it's alongside others who've also been born again. As we celebrate being rescued in the ark, as it were, protected by God's mercy and grace from the desolation outside, we find ourselves there with others who've also entered through the One door. We can each enjoy amazing personal access to God, but He also wants His children to join together at times in worship before His throne.

So when we consider a situation in which people are being exposed to God's Word, and we try to gauge whether they have a growing understanding of their true identity from God's perspective, it's not only about them as individuals. We would also be listening for indications that they have some sense of themselves as individual children of God within His family. It would certainly be a positive sign that Truth was being shared effectively if they were to speak about how God sees them *in Christ* along with everyone else who has put their faith in Him.

On the other hand, it would cause us real concern to find that the person's primary identity as a Christian seemed to be all about church or denominational affiliation; if they continually related their faith to a cultural or family tradition, to social obligation, to "going to church", rather than to personal, but shared, understanding, conviction and relationship with the Lord.

A final thought. As we consider how we can assess a situation in which God's Word is being shared (personal discipleship, small group, a church, etc.), we are not suggesting that we assume a sense of superiority, habitually critiquing every such situation we come across. First and foremost, this W.I.L.D. framework is intended to give us categories and resources for evaluating efforts to share God's Word that we are personally involved in.

On the other hand, we often do find ourselves needing to consider something being described or a situation we're observing first-hand. As we discussed in the introductory tutorials, there are numerous models for evangelism and church planting out there, and more being developed all the time. And it is important that we have in mind some areas that we believe are consistent with God's purposes when strategies are suggested or when claims are made. Hopefully we're convinced that whoever is sharing with who, whatever the form it takes, the context, the time-frames, the numbers, the circumstances...the sharing of God's Word should result in people becoming increasingly clear about, and able to articulate, their true identity from God's perspective.

Some extra questions

To go along with the first question in the area of *Identity*, 'Are they increasingly clear about - and able to articulate - their true identity from God's perspective?', we can also ask:

- Are they having their assumptions about who they are challenged and shaped by God's Word as it reveals who He is, how He sees needy human beings, and the implications of what Jesus accomplished on the Cross?
- Are they able to explain that they've been given a new life and identity in Christ, totally through the work of God's Spirit, and not through any inherent worthiness of their own?
- Are they realizing that although they are individual children of God, they are also a part of His family - a corporate identity defined by a shared relationship with Jesus Christ?

UNDERSTANDING TRUE IDENTITY

❓ DISCUSSION POINTS

1. When you read the Bible are you very conscious of what it is saying about who you are? Have you ever, for example, read one of the New Testament epistles looking specifically through that lens; i.e. what is being expressed (either directly or assumed) about the identity of God the Father, Son and Spirit, the author, the original recipients, believers, unbelievers, the Church, yourself? Any thoughts about this?

2. Consider some of the groups you are part of and try to identify the boundaries that define each of them. What determines membership? Who are the "us" and who are "them"?

3. For someone in our society hearing God's Word taught clearly for the first time, what do you think might be some of the obstacles in their worldview that might prevent them coming to a clear understanding of how God sees them?

➡ ACTIVITIES

1. Look for opportunities to talk to someone about their sense of self, who they see themselves to be, as an individual and as part of any groups they feel they belong to. If possible, have this conversation with an unbeliever and a believer. Then record any observations you care to about:

- How difficult you found it to get into conversations about this topic.
- The kinds of things you said and the questions you asked to open up the conversation.
- Any insights you gained through the process.

7.12 The Narrative of the Church

 OBJECTIVES OF THIS TUTORIAL

This tutorial continues to discuss the area of *Identity*, and looks at the second question in that area: 'Are they learning to see their story embedded in the larger Narrative of the Church, stretching back to Pentecost and forward to Christ's return?'

Last time

We moved into the next W.I.L.D. area of Identity and began to grapple with this complex and potentially abstract concept. We thought about how even in brief encounters we use what are often subconscious categories to identify people…also that, intentionally or not, we are always projecting something about who we see ourselves to be. We also touched briefly on how our individual identity is linked to the groups we're a part of… and the way these different groups are determined by their boundaries. We then looked at the first question under "I" for Identity and considered what kinds of things would indicate that someone's view of their identity was being aligned to who God says they are.

The second question under "I" for *Identity*

- Are they increasingly clear about - and able to articulate - their true identity from God's perspective?

- <u>Are they learning to see their story embedded in the larger Narrative of the Church, stretching back to Pentecost and forward to Christ's return?</u>

- Are they growing in their understanding of the bonds that unite them to the global/local Body under Christ as its Head?

- Are they learning to view others according to truth, and rejecting the divisions, biases and tensions that often define the wider society?

- Are they growing in their understanding of how to appropriately represent the Lord in their current spheres of contact and in others He might lead them to be involved in?

You'll certainly be aware by now, particularly if you've engaged with Modules 1 and 2 in the *AccessTruth Curriculum*, of the importance we place on the description of God as Author and the Bible as His Narrative. We've discussed a number of reasons for that, but we want to explore it again here in light of this current topic - an individual and a group of believers gaining clarity about how to define who they are based on God's perspective.

Our identity in His

Implicit in Satan's lie to human beings in the beginning and ever since, is that "like gods" - like small creators and authors in our own right - we can say who we actually are, and are able to shape an identity for ourselves as individuals and communities. He says that we can find our place in the universe and say, "This is who I am" or, "This is who we are." The reality of course is that we don't have an identity or a story of our own. It's only against the backdrop of who God is, as He reveals Himself to us, that we have an identity and can know who we actually are. So when someone comes to faith and then grows on to maturity, it can be described as a process of them learning who they are as individuals within Christ's Ecclesia.

When someone suffers from amnesia, they lose part of their own story: either a brief moment, an episode, or even whole chunks of memories from their past. In extreme cases, known as *fugue*, there is a total loss of identity, often involving the person physically running away from their normal environment. (The word fugue comes from the Latin 'fuga' for *flight*.)

A famous case of fugue, and one of the first documented, was the real man who Jason Bourne - from the Ludlum books and popular movies - was named after. In 1887 Ansel Bourne, a preacher from Rhode Island, USA, was supposed to go and visit his sister's house a few miles away. Instead, without any memory of how it happened, he woke up one morning two months later, over 300 kilometers away in Pennsylvania, shocked to find he'd used all his savings to open a variety store there under the name Albert J. Brown.

Whether from physical trauma or physiological causes, people experiencing amnesia or the more extreme fugue have their personal stories disrupted, and this has significant results for their sense of identity. Something related happens when people migrate voluntarily to find 'a better life', or when they're suddenly forced to flee their homes as refugees. They often experience dislocation from the assumptions of selfhood they've always had. As time goes by, the personal and societal narratives that gave them a sense of security become less and less applicable. They no longer fit into the individual and corporate identity from their original community, and often never really fit into where they settle either, because the history of this new country and society is not theirs.

The apostle Paul told the believers in Corinth that, "...anyone who belongs to Christ has become a new person. The old life is gone; a new life has begun!" (2 Corinthians 5:17). The plot line of their lives had taken a radical, irreversible turn. There is a disconnect between who they used to be before coming to faith in Jesus Christ and who they will be from now on.

In his letter to "God's chosen people" who were part of the Jewish diaspora in the Roman provinces of modern day Turkey, Peter says that they once lived in darkness *without an identity* (1 Peter 2:9-12), Now God has brought them into His light where they have an identity, purpose, and meaningful roles. Yes, they look the same, live in the same houses, eat the same food, but they're different. They have been given full membership in a people group that's defined by much more important things than human language, ethnicity and history. Their lives now tell a story that is totally different to the accepted cultural narratives of their unbelieving friends, families and neighbors.

Usman's Story

My name is Usman. I live in the foothills of the Hindu Kush mountain range. A while ago I got to know a foreigner from Switzerland who stayed in town for a year as part of a clean water aid project. We first met when this guy, Philippe, came into my small bicycle repair shop to buy a new tire. Then he started dropping by regularly to drink tea and practice speaking Khowar, my language. After a while we started talking about religious matters and eventually we began studying the Holy Books of Tawrat (the Torah), and Injil (the Gospels). I came to believe with all my heart that Isa (Jesus) is God's Son, the true, final prophet...and His death is the only sacrifice for sin that God can accept.

The Swiss guy is gone now, and life has certainly become more challenging. So far, at least my brothers haven't been violent as some might be to demonstrate their own piety, but I'm certainly no longer welcome at family gatherings. For a time I kept attending the mosque, but increasingly I felt like a stranger there and seldom go now, even on Fridays. I used to be a regular at the monthly gatherings of the town's businessmen, but a delegation of former friends came around to my shop a while back and told me to stay away. At first my wife was bitter about my new faith and threatened to take our daughter back to her mother's place in a village across the river, but I've tried to treat her with love and respect and lately she's been asking questions. There's no translation of the Bible in Khowar but I read it in Urdu even though I don't understand everything in that language.

The hardest thing though is...how do I explain it? It's a sense of no longer belonging to anything. Of being cut off. Of feeling like I no longer really fit anywhere. I ask myself who I am now. Most of the ways I would once have described myself to a stranger no longer seem accurate. People here call me Murtid an apostate, and a Nasraani, a Christian, but they mean a follower of a western religion and culture, with many bad connotations. That's not who I am. I've heard there are churches in some cities, but I've never been to one. Recently I got talking with an older couple here in town who I think might believe in Isa, Jesus. Maybe we can meet sometimes. Philippe, the aid worker, taught me that I am a child of God, a disciple of Isa...but he left before I felt I fully understood what that means. I pray to God to help me understand who I am and what I belong to now.

The identity of the early Church

The book of Acts in many ways is a story of identity. It starts out with a small group of people, mostly from a Jewish cultural and religious background, and many with regional (Galilean) connections. But their primary distinction was that they were followers of an itinerant Rabbi, a Teacher, who they were sure was the long-awaited Messiah, the Son of God. After His return to Heaven, this small band stayed on in Jerusalem, as He'd instructed. Clearly there was some sense of common identity, but it wasn't until after the Holy Spirit arrived on the day of Pentecost that they really began to have a presence in the community as a distinct group.

They are immediately forced to deal with the reality of being a minority group within a larger unbelieving and increasingly hostile community. They wrestle with issues of identity. Baptism and celebrating the Lord's Supper are important symbolic practices that help to define them. But what does it mean, exactly, to be people of this New Covenant? Who are *God's chosen people* now? How can you be a Jew and also follower of Jesus? Should they attend temple ceremonies? How should they define themselves in Jerusalem, or in the outlying regions of Israel? Certainly they are followers of Jesus, but should anything else define and distinguish them as sharing a common identity? And, as the Gospel spreads around the Mediterranean, how should believers relate to the Jewish synagogue system, to Greek philosophy, the Roman Empire, to animistic, pagan neighbors?

The great comfort is that they are not left alone to wrestle with these issues. All the time, God is continuing to reveal Truth and unfold His Story for them. As Jesus promised, the Holy Spirit is with each of them, and with them as a Group, a Church. He's giving special prophetic insights to chosen individuals who speak on God's behalf to the Church; being a New Covenant believer means having access to God's ongoing revelation. The teaching of the apostles itself represents a defining, distinguishing feature for individuals, for local ecclesia, and for the entire Church. Just as the writings of Moses and the prophets defined God's people under the Old Covenant, access to the verbal, then written, teaching of the apostles defines the new Ecclesia.

At the same time, through the apostles' teaching, God is making very specific declarations to these believers about *who* they are. And as we've already noted, identity is inextricably linked to purpose. At the beginning of his first letter to the believers in Corinth, Paul says that God has called them His *holy people*. And their purpose? They are intended to live and work in partnership with His Son, Jesus Christ. To the Ephesians, the apostle writes that they are members of the *Body of Christ* with the goal of reaching individual and corporate maturity (Ephesians 4:12-13). The early churches are told they are *God's temple*, a place for His Spirit to live on earth. A living *letter* from God through which He communicates to the community. They are *witnesses*, *light*, *salt*, *living sacrifices*. And there's a future component to their identity and purpose as well. They are the *Bride* of God's Son, the *New Jerusalem*, made to be His perfect companion, to give glory to their Redeemer and Lord for eternity.

A connected identity

Hopefully the connections between the insights God gave the early Church to deal with the identity issues that perplexed them, and the similar issues facing a new believer or church today are obvious. Our second question under "I" for *Identity* prompts us to consider whether they are *"learning to see their story embedded in the larger Narrative of the Church."* Just like the first believers in Jerusalem or Colossae, a young Christian today, whether in London or a small town in the Hindu Kush, faces the reality of disconnection from their past, dislocation from their place in their community, and disorientation in identity. Fellowship with others in a similar situation is obviously important, but it is also possible - in fact very common - for groups of believers never to really come to the right conclusions about who they are or why they are even there.

People can't exist in an 'identity vacuum': i.e. without some perception of who they are. Physiologically disturbed individuals are said to be suffering from *fugue* because they've created fictional identities, histories, and purposes for living. They have a compelling need to function within some conceptual framework of themselves, even if it bears no relationship to reality.

Likewise, a church that isn't growing in their understanding about how God sees them, that hasn't seriously engaged with what the apostles taught the early Church about their identity, that has no sense of being directly connected into God's Narrative of the Church, won't exist somehow without any self-perception. They will function on the basis of assumptions about their identity, but if their perspectives are not being actively shaped by God's cohesive true Story of the past, present and future of the Church, their assumptions will be wrong. The way they see themselves and their purpose for existence will unconsciously be influenced by the categories and stories of the larger culture. They'll distinguish themselves by outward forms: the kind of building they meet in, how they conduct their services, even how they dress...or perhaps they will focus on certain practices or denominational distinctives...or numerous other ways of identifying themselves that at best are secondary or negotiable, and at worst are completely wrong.

On the other hand, individuals and churches that are "learning to see their story embedded in the larger Narrative of the Church" are being equipped to identify themselves correctly. They don't see themselves and their church as an end in itself...they understand that God has placed them there at that place and time in history to play a role within His overall purposes for the Church. They see the Narrative of the Church as directly relating to who they are and how they should relate to each other and to those who are not yet God's children. They share the most fundamental and important aspects of identity with the early Church as God revealed through the apostles. They are understanding that other distinctives should serve their primary identity as the Building, Body and Bride of Christ.

Some extra questions

To go along with the second question under *Identity*, 'Are they learning to see their story embedded in the larger Narrative of the Church, stretching back to Pentecost and forward to Christ's return?', we can also ask;

- Is the shared experience of growing through the teaching of Jesus and His apostles itself forming a part of their identity as a local body of His disciples?
- Do they have access to teaching from the New Testament account that clearly shows how the truth given to the early Church also provides them with all the foundational Truth for dealing with their own identity issues?
- Do they have a growing sense of who they are and why they exist as a group of God's children in that particular place in ways that tie in with the Church's story, past, present and future?

❓ DISCUSSION POINTS

1. Share anything you care to about your own experience of coming to terms with your identity as a Christian. Would you say that you often tend to think of yourself and your personal story as being connected back to the early days of the Church? Has your experience of engaging with God's Word in the past encouraged this view or not really?

2. When most people in the West think of Christians and the Church, what do you think comes to mind? How have the "stories" of our culture (books, movies, media, internet etc.) played into this perception? In general, what would you say has been the response of the Church to the way it has been characterized by the larger community?

➡ ACTIVITIES

1. In Acts Chapter 9 find at least four of the ways the early believers are referred to. Share any thoughts you have on each of the names or terms of reference you come across.

7.13 One Body in Christ

 OBJECTIVES OF THIS TUTORIAL

This tutorial continues to discuss the area of *Identity*, and looks at the third question in that area: 'Are they growing in their understanding of the bonds that unite them to the global/local Body under Christ as its Head?'

Last time

We drew a parallel between the physiological condition known as *fugue* and the potential for confusion about identity and purpose that can happen for a new believer, as they become new people in Christ.

We remembered how the early Church, trying to understand its place in the past, present and future, were given answers by God's Spirit through the apostles' teaching. This clarified their identity and purpose from God's true perspective.

Individuals and groups of believers today need to see how that Narrative and the Truth it contains is also relevant to them in their own time and place. In fact, they need to see this as *their* story, *their* identity and *their* purpose. It is how they can have a healthy view of where they come from, why they exist now, and where they are going.

The third question under "I" for *Identity*

- Are they increasingly clear about - and able to articulate - their true identity from God's perspective?
- Are they learning to see their story embedded in the larger Narrative of the Church, stretching back to Pentecost and forward to Christ's return?
- <u>Are they growing in their understanding of the bonds that unite them to the global/local Body under Christ as its Head?</u>
- Are they learning to view others according to truth, and rejecting the divisions, biases and tensions that often define the wider society?
- Are they growing in their understanding of how to appropriately represent the

Lord in their current spheres of contact and in others He might lead them to be involved in?

In previous tutorials we've touched on the fact that people's cultural story, their *worldview*, has enormous potential for impacting the way they view themselves as individual believers and as a church. This is particularly so for the issues we're considering in this third question under *Identity*: what a church understands unites it, and how they perceive authority. Worldview will also be relevant for the fourth question, which asks how well they avoid the negative aspects of sub-group identities that dog most communities (e.g. gaps related to age, gender, financial and social status, education, family or clan, etc.).

Existing cultural values

AccessTruth Module 4 presents some cultural scales that give us ways of defining some related areas of culture. Here, very briefly, are four that are very relevant to the subject of identity in the church (for fuller explanations see Tutorials 4.7, 4.9 and 4.13).

Note that these kinds of definitions force us to speak in generalities while, in reality, cultures are much more nuanced, with many 'exceptions to the rule'. But there is value in looking for the common threads and considering how, unless submitted to the authority of God's Word, those cultural threads can create inbuilt weaknesses for the church (See *Tutorial 7.8*). Also note that no extreme in any spectrum is inherently healthier or more positive than the other extreme. Only in Jesus Christ Himself do we find a human being who embodied the perfect balance in all areas and was entirely pleasing to the Father.

1. Individualism vs. Collectivism:

Individualism: people are focused on themselves and their personal needs; self-sufficiency and self-reliance are highly valued; people identify themselves individually rather than as part of a group.

Collectivism: identities are primarily group related; success of the group ensures the well being of the individual; visible harmony and interdependence are valued; closeness within the group often means distance towards non-group members.

2. Universalism vs. Particularism:

Universalism: applies accepted "absolutes" to everyone, regardless of the circumstances of relationships; "fairness" is treating everyone the same; it values looking at a situation "objectively".

Particularism: circumstances, rightfully, change behavior; there are no absolutes because right and wrong is determined by who you're dealing with - by relationships; exceptions can always be made to rules.

3. High Power Distance vs. Low Power Distance:

High Power Distance: accepts the inevitability of inequalities in power and status; power is held close, not shared; distinctions are accentuated, but the powerful are expected to look after subordinates.

Low Power Distance: inequalities in status are considered artificial, just a matter of convenience; distinctions are minimized; initiative is valued and rewarded.

4. Achieved Status vs. Ascribed Status:

Achieved Status: positions of influence are reached through accomplishment, rather than family background or connections; status is earned and can be lost through poor performance.

Ascribed Status: prestige is inherent in the person and is difficult to lose; power is often automatic and is related to social class, affiliations or age; titles are important.

Time and space here doesn't allow us to detail the numerous ways that a church can unthinkingly adopt the values of the wider community as far as its sense of identity; but even a brief glimpse at these four sample scales should show that individual and collective cultural assumptions have a huge potential impact.

A church, for example, whose members come from a very *individualistic* society might well struggle to really have a sense of being bonded together as a group. Where *collectivism*, on the other hand, is the cultural norm, church members can value a surface harmony and apparent unity that is not really built on the things that God says actually do tie them together. In a culture that downplays *power distance* and insists that *status must be achieved*, church members may struggle to recognise authority, even an appropriate authority delegated by God's Spirit to gifted individuals. By contrast, in a community where *power distance is high* and *status is ascribed*, church leadership can be very strong, but it may not be established on Biblical authority, instead being assigned according to cultural norms of status, age, family connections, wealth etc.

God's values

The solution to the potential imbalances and weaknesses that can bleed over into the church from its surrounding culture is, of course, to allow God's values to shape our thinking. As the apostle Paul said in his letter to the believers in Rome (Romans 12:2), "Don't copy the behavior and customs of this world, but let God transform you into a new person by changing the way you think." The need to be transformed in our thinking is just as relevant to our view of our identity as it is to any other area of life. What's true for us as individuals is also true for the way an entire group sees itself; and specifically this issue we're considering of what actually ties them together, what are the bonds, the "glue" that even makes them a local body? Hopefully we are completely convinced by now that this transformation comes about through God's Word being communicated clearly, cohesively and in ways that are relevant to previously unexamined areas of worldview, beliefs, values and day-to-day behavior.

Back in Tutorial 7.11, in the introduction to the whole area of *Identity*, we very briefly considered different kinds of groups. We noted then that there are many different kinds, that *purpose* has a great deal to do with identity, and that the way *boundaries* are viewed is also critical. Another hugely important factor that comes into focus here is *authority* - who or what has the right to define what the group is, how it is distinct, the way it should function and how it should relate to others who are not part of the group?

Take an example. If we think of a nation, a country, as an example of a group, we can define it in a number of ways: by its geographical boundaries, ethnic make-up, cultural features etc. But think how important it is - in terms of the way a country sees itself and is seen by others - *who* actually holds the power to influence and control. In a democracy that power is, at least theoretically, in the hands of the majority who elect representatives to govern them. (Of course that's not the whole story, with the media, financial institutions, lobbyists etc. also exerting significant influence in Western democracies.) And then there are various shades of more authoritarian systems in which a ruling elite or even a single individual holds power. To take some random and widely contrasting examples, consider the impact the issue of authority has on the ways that North Korea, Saudi Arabia, Denmark and Russia respectively see themselves and their place in the world.

But what about *the* Church, or *a* church? Obviously the issue of where authority is seen to be - not only in a theoretical or doctrinal way but also in a very real, practical sense - will have a critical impact on the way that group views itself. Are they, for example, defined and held together by a church constitution? Or a doctrinal statement? A denominational structure? Maybe through the strength and charisma of an individual? None of these are inherently wrong, in fact they can be very helpful for the life of a church, but ultimately it *is* a church group, a body (and part of the universal Body), only because of the Headship of Christ. It exists as an extension of His will, His intent. It was born through His sacrifice. Its true identity is a product of its relationship to Him. Anything else that might contribute to the church's identity has to be subsidiary to this. It can only have validity if it is clarifying and pointing toward Christ as its Head. The influence any individual has within the church is only appropriate if they are leading others to know more of Him and to understand His purposes.

Let's remember that our objective in these Tutorials is to determine how we can best evaluate a situation in which Truth is being shared. So in terms of Identity, what kinds of things would we want to hear in conversations with people? What would encourage us that they are, as this third question says, "growing in their understanding of the bonds that unite them to the global/local Body under Christ as its Head?" Well, we'd love to hear evidence that the way they see themselves as a group is dominated by a consciousness of Christ as their one Lord, as in Paul's words to the Ephesians (Ephesians 4:4-6). As well as that, we'd be reassured that Truth was being effectively shared with them if they mentioned some of the other things Paul referred to in that same part of his letter…that they are tied together as a body by God's Spirit, by their shared faith, by their baptism that symbolizes their identity with Jesus' death and resurrection, and by an amazing future they can picture themselves sharing with the rest of His people.

Some extra questions

To go along with the third question in the area of *Identity*, 'Are they growing in their understanding of the bonds that unite them to the global/local Body under Christ as its Head?', we can also ask;

- Are they allowing God's Word to define the proper basis of their relationships as a group, or are they unknowingly applying the values of the wider culture in the church context?
- Is there a sense that anything or anyone's authority to shape who they are as a church is legitimate if, and only if, it actively recognises Christ as the true Head of the Body?
- Whatever other factors might also draw them together, is it ultimately their shared faith, hope and identity in Christ that they see tying them together and defining them as a local church body?

Read the conversation below and then answer the following questions.

(The opinions expressed by the fictional characters are their own and don't necessarily reflect our own.)

Andrew: Hey Liam, I haven't seen you for a while, how are things?

Liam: Yeah, good to see you again Andrew. I got a new job and moved out to the northern suburbs.

Andrew: I guess that's why our paths haven't crossed at church. You still go there, right?

Liam: Actually I don't any more. I must admit, I was a bit sick of it after three years.

Andrew: Oh really…like what?

Liam: Well, the music and the worship style didn't suit me that much. And I don't know…they seem really into like, doctrine and stuff. Not my thing.

Andrew: What about Emma? I though I saw her at church recently.

Liam: Oh, yeah, she sometimes comes with me on Saturday night, but she still often goes over to your church on Sunday mornings. Not sure what we'll do when we get married.

Andrew: Okay, well I didn't really hear that you'd left. Was it like…did you mention it to Gary or anything?

Liam: The main pastor guy? No, I didn't know him very well. In all the time I was going there I reckon I only spoke to him once or twice. He's from overseas and he doesn't seem into sport or music, so I didn't know what we'd talk about. I did get a call from the church office…apparently someone noticed I hadn't been for over a month. I appreciated them making the effort.

Andrew: So where are you going now?

Liam: It's a kind of a mega-church offshoot near where I live now. They're right into the music and worship, as you'd expect. They don't make that big a deal about the preaching. But there's a lot of pressure to get involved in outreaches and charity stuff… that kind of bugs me. Guess it's okay. I think they see it as part of their branding.

Andrew: *Hey, I heard about this group that meets at a pub in the city…I think on Thursday nights. They use the barbecue facilities and then have a Bible study one of the rooms. Apparently it's pretty good. Sounds like most of the people aren't really church type Christians. Maybe you'd like it. They've got a website. I'll forward you the link if you want.*

Liam: *Okay, cool. Yeah, Emma and I might check it out. Better run. See ya.*

Andrew: *Let's catch up for a coffee again some time. Bye.*

❓ DISCUSSION POINTS

1. Make any general comments you care to about Liam's view of "church". Try to keep in mind the points we've been discussing so far about Identity.

2. Can you identify anything about Liam's attitudes that might be shaped by the assumptions of his culture? (Note the four cultural scales from the tutorial.)

3. If you had opportunity to share God's Word with Liam in a regular Bible study, how would you set about trying to address some of the gaps in his understanding of Identity issues that you might have noticed in his conversation with Andrew?

4. What are your thoughts about Andrew suggesting that Liam and his fiancée try the Bible study in the pub? Explain why you do or don't think it was a good idea for Andrew to suggest that as an alternative to their current church experience.

7.14 Viewing others according to truth

 OBJECTIVES OF THIS TUTORIAL

This tutorial continues to discuss the area of *Identity*, and looks at the fourth and fifth questions in that area: 'Are they learning to view others according to truth, and rejecting the divisions, biases and tensions that often define the wider society?' and 'Are they growing in their understanding of how to appropriately represent the Lord in their current spheres of contact and in others He might lead them to be involved in?'

Last time

We considered the potential impact a person's worldview and cultural assumptions have on their view of *Identity*, as individuals and as part of a church body. We identified four relevant aspects of culture - Individualism vs. Collectivism, Universalism vs. Particularism, High vs. Low Power Distance, Achieved vs. Ascribed Status - and briefly considered how assumptions in these areas impact a view of identity and authority. We noted that it is only through believers submitting to the authority of God's Word that their ingrained attitudes can be challenged and aligned to His perspective on these issues...to see with the kind of perspective Paul described to the Ephesians, "...there is one body and one Spirit...one glorious hope...one Lord, one faith, one baptism."

The fourth question under "I" for *Identity*

- Are they increasingly clear about - and able to articulate - their true identity from God's perspective?
- Are they learning to see their story embedded in the larger Narrative of the Church, stretching back to Pentecost and forward to Christ's return?
- Are they growing in their understanding of the bonds that unite them to the global/local Body under Christ as its Head?
- <u>Are they learning to view others according to truth, and rejecting the divisions, biases and tensions that often define the wider society?</u>
- Are they growing in their understanding of how to appropriately represent the Lord in their current spheres of contact and in others He might lead them to be involved in?

The previous question dealt with an individual or group's *theoretical* grasp of what ties a church together; now we want to deal with some more practical areas related to how much unity (or fragmentation) is being *experienced* within the diversity of a local body. We noted the danger of cultural assumptions shaping the way members of a church perceive their own place, and the place of authority, within a group. We talked about the need for God to transform their thinking, their "mind" in this area.

As we consider this fourth *Identity* question - how different sub-groups within a church relate to each other - it's obvious that this transformative power of God's Word is no less important here as well. The pride and self-obsession of individual human hearts finds its collective expression in the tensions and divisions that plague every country and community. It's only through the careful teaching and application of Truth that a church body can hope to recognise and avoid the inbuilt tensions that can be so destructive.

A common identity with Him

When Paul wrote to the churches in the highland province of Galatia - what is now part of modern day Turkey - he was addressing issues of identity as they wrestled with what it meant to be God's children under the New Covenant. What were the implications for the Jewish and Gentile believers in the congregations? And what were the differences between them? The apostle explains (Galatians 3:26-28) that through faith they've all been so closely associated with Jesus Christ - as represented by baptism - that it's not possible to tell them apart from Him. Their common identity with Him is complete. And so all the other things that they once defined themselves by, and which came between them - things like ethnicity, social status and gender - those have all now become redundant, subsumed into this new identity they share with Christ and with each other.

Of course as we picture a situation in which we might one day share God's Word, or if we're 'taking the pulse' of something already in existence, it's unlikely that we'll come across tensions between Jewish vs. Gentile cultural identities. But there are numerous other potential sources of tension and conflict that build weaknesses into the church, negatively impact its testimony, and can even cause its eventual disintegration. In the face of this reality, Paul told the Ephesian believers that they'd need to learn patience (Ephesians 4:2,3). It wasn't that they wouldn't be likely to notice shortcomings in each other.

The default for human beings is to see themselves as being the bar by which everyone else is judged, with others usually falling well short. This is also true for whatever groupings people use to define themselves: "Those people are not quite as cool, not as smart, not as good as us." Or, "Those people think they're so cool, so smart, so good!" There are an infinite number of ways to divide and diverge, to segregate and separate. Overcoming those defaults, Paul tells the Ephesians that it is going to take work, real effort… they have to remember that their natural view of other people and sub-groups within the church as separate and, no doubt, inferior to themselves, is a faulty view. The reality is they are united by God's Spirit who lives in each of them, who *indwells* the whole Body of Christ. So they have to put effort into eliminating perspectives that divide and create tensions, instead focusing on the fundamental truths about who they are that bring genuine harmony.

What might we find to indicate a church is *not* applying Truth in these areas of identity? Of course we should never expect to find perfect harmony, but what would suggest the presence of a serious fragmentation between different sub-groups in the church that is likely to inhibit growth and fruit? We might find a strong sense of separation between the young and the old, for example. Or perhaps the men are domineering and dismissive of the important contribution women can make in the life and outreach of the church. Is there a feeling of conflict in the air, of agendas being pushed, or even just an indifferent ignorance about the daily experiences of others? Is the health and growth of the church seen to be the concern of just a few? In certain cultural settings we might find fracture lines that follow family or clan lines. Maybe church members are lining up behind different charismatic leaders ("I'm of Paul." "I'm of Apollos."). Are people playing politics, lobbying for their special interests, getting together to criticize leaders, using social media to fuel divisions?

Sadly the list of negative factors that can fracture a church is endless, but the solution is always the same; believers having opportunity to respond to God's Spirit as Truth is applied coherently and consistently within the reality of their lives. And a critically important theme that has to keep emerging from God's Word, His Narrative, is who *He says* they are - as individuals and as a group - against the backdrop of who He always is.

A final point about this issue of how much the "divisions, biases and tensions" of the larger community are replicated in the church: in a situation where Truth is being shared in a community with the goal of seeing a new fellowship established, the approach of the church planters themselves can have long lasting and widespread implications.

A great deal, in fact, always rests on how much those who are sharing God's Word have allowed Him to shape their own sense of identity. This plays out in real willingness, commitments and even courage in building relationships. If they are only prepared to pursue meaningful connections with people who they feel comfortable with - those of a similar age, who share the same interests, who are not intimidating, etc. - then in all likelihood the church-to-be will have inbuilt limitations. A church that starts with people drawn mainly from one age bracket, ethnic sub-group, socio-economic class, or even gender, *can* grow past that stage and eventually have a congregation that more fairly represents wider demographics. But the more different kinds of people make up a church from the outset, the better placed it will be to attract others and be the vital witness God intends it to be in the community.

Some extra questions

To go along with the fourth question under *Identity*, 'Are they learning to view others according to truth, and rejecting the divisions, biases and tensions that often define the wider society?', we can also ask:

- Are they increasingly less concerned about perceived differences with brothers and sisters from other cultural sub-groups, instead learning to focus on the more fundamental common identity they have as members of Christ's body?
- Are they learning to value diversity within the body, respecting and appreciating the role of others regardless of gender, age, education, social status, wealth, etc.?
- Are they committed to reaching out to everyone, regardless of any ingrained prejudices in the society, so that people from all the different levels and sub-groups have access to God's Word and to the life of the church?

The fifth question under "I" for *Identity*

- Are they increasingly clear about - and able to articulate - their true identity from God's perspective?
- Are they learning to see their story embedded in the larger Narrative of the Church, stretching back to Pentecost and forward to Christ's return?
- Are they growing in their understanding of the bonds that unite them to the global/local Body under Christ as its Head?
- Are they learning to view others according to truth, and rejecting the divisions, biases and tensions that often define the wider society?
- <u>Are they growing in their understanding of how to appropriately represent the Lord in their current spheres of contact and in others He might lead them to be involved in?</u>

God's intention for Israel as a people was always clear. He told Abraham that he'd be the father of a nation *through which all other nations would be blessed* (Genesis 12:3). Later, laying out for Moses the terms of the Covenant that defined Israel as His people, He said that through them He'd demonstrate His power to the surrounding nations (Exodus 34:10). They were intended to be His witnesses (Isaiah 43:10). To demonstrate the incredible blessing of having access to God's Word (Deuteronomy 4:6,33). Even though they failed many times to be what God intended, this role of being a light and a witness, of being the means of God's communication and blessing to others…this was built into their DNA. It was who they were as a people, whether they recognized it or not.

We've talked before about *purpose* having very close links to *identity*. In terms of identity/purpose, what was true for God's people under the First Covenant is also true for those defined by the Second. But God's outreach role for this new people would be even clearer, wider in scope, and carrying more authority than was the case for Israel. The Founder of this Group was, Himself, *the Word*, God's Revelation in human form. The men He chose, equipped and commissioned to continue building the church were apostles, *sent-out ones*. The mandate they received directly from Him, and that they'd pass on to others, was to *go out*, to be His *witnesses everywhere*. The pattern He described was of His people moving out with Truth from an initial local base in ever-widening circles.

From its inauguration on the Jewish feast day of Pentecost, God's Spirit empowered the fledgling Church to move out like that, certainly geographically but also across boundaries of prejudice, worldview, ethnicity and even language. The Narrative of the early Church in the centuries that followed was one of expansion, of taking God's Truth into new areas, of being exactly *who* He said it was. It was not without an enormous cost being paid by the obedient ones; because being identified with the One who gave Himself as a sacrifice, means being a sacrifice yourself. And not without problems and failures, regular losses of focus and confusion about the purpose, and enormous struggles to keep the integrity of the Truth. But despite that, God's Spirit has continued to use His Word and those He's raised up over the last 2000 years to remind His Church who it is and why it exists in the world. (By the way, it should be clear that we're not talking about the geopolitical power-seeking of any man-made institution that wrongly calls itself *The Church* here, but rather the Body of Christ that has stayed true to the Gospel of His Grace as the apostles recorded it, and as it has been passed on from one generation of His children to the next.)

That purpose-linked identity of the *universal* Church, the *Ecclesia*, is also true of *local* gatherings of His people. Just as the concept of being witnesses and ambassadors; of having an innate purpose beyond itself as a group; of being people who looked by faith for something greater and further on…in the same way that was essential to the founding of the Church back then, it should also resonate as a consistent theme whenever there's opportunity to share God's Narrative with any individual or group today. In the second question under *Identity* we focused on the need for people to see their story embedded in the larger Narrative of the Church. When this happens, a direct link is forged between their own emerging identity and the formative experience of the early Church as it came to terms with who it was in light of its mission.

Living out our identity

Our fifth *Identity* question, however, is focused not only on an individual or group's sense of purpose-in-identity, but also about how *appropriately* they are living that out. Do they know - or are they learning - not only that they *are* disciple witnesses, but also *how* to be relevant in that role? What does it mean, for example, to be a representative of Jesus in a society where there's a church on every corner and most people call themselves Christians? How can you live out your true identity as a Christian if you're a student in an aggressively secular, pluralistic academic setting? How can you be a courageous witness for the Lord when your family and friends believe you're a traitor to your religion and country? Is it even possible to be an authentic believer in a cut-throat corporate business environment? In practical terms, how can you be a light when you and everyone else in the community are desperately poor and barely able to find enough to eat? How can you be a relevant Christian on social media without making everyone you know "*unfriend*" or "*unfollow*" you? What does it look like to be a disciple of Christ at sea for weeks at a time on a fishing trawler?

These are the kinds of questions that followers of Christ should be wrestling with and finding answers for in God's Word. Not that there are any simple formulas to follow. But if Truth is being shared effectively with anyone, then by definition it is not only clarifying in a theoretical or "doctrinal" sense *who* they are in their new life, but it is also equipping them to live out that identity in the reality of their daily situations.

And what's true for individuals is also true for a group of God's children. Whether it's a new church or one that has been around for decades, they should be continuing to grow "in their understanding of how to appropriately represent the Lord" in their community. They should learn to ask, and find answers from God's Word to, questions like these: *If it's true, as we're realizing, that Christ has intentionally drawn us together as a group of His disciples/witnesses here, what does that mean in real terms? What are the implications for where we should meet together and when? We know that there's every chance that people will have assumptions about us based on their previous experiences with "religion" and "church": so what - if anything - should we do about that? How should we be trying to present ourselves in the community? What should be our relationship with the local authorities, with institutions, with other churches? What should feature on our website as our online face?* And so on...

So we could say that as a person or church comes to understand who they are *in Christ* and *in His Body*, they are also learning who they are *in the world*. And the borders of that "world" should continue to grow. Initially, as a new believer or church glimpses what it truly means to be a witness of Jesus, many are concerned - and rightly so - with their immediate family, friends, neighborhood and community. Gradually though, they should begin to look out from that sphere of contact with a widening view. God loves the *world*. He is certainly concerned for those closest to us, but He is equally concerned for His entire harvest field. He wants everyone to have the opportunity to turn to Him in faith. So a growing clarity about what it means to be His servants, individually and corporately, means an increasingly global view of what that service entails.

If we find ourselves needing to assess a strategy for sharing God's Word that someone is proposing, or if we're picturing our own future contribution, perhaps evaluating progress of a situation we're currently involved in, or if we're wanting to gauge the health of a church no matter how new or old…we should be looking for an outward trajectory. Is it resulting in them knowing how to represent the Lord where they currently are and then into broader contexts as He leads?

Some extra questions

To go along with the fifth question under *Identity*, 'Are they growing in their understanding of how to appropriately represent the Lord in their current spheres of contact and in others He might lead them to be involved in?', we can also ask:

- As they engage with Truth, are they understanding God's intention for them to live out their identities as His witnesses to their families, friends and community?
- Are they wrestling with the practical realities of what it means to be relevant representatives of Christ in their particular contexts?
- Is their growing understanding of being God's servants resulting in an expanding view of "the world" and the role they can play in giving others access to the Gospel?

VIEWING OTHERS ACCORDING TO TRUTH

? DISCUSSION POINTS

1. In your own cultural context, what are some of the existing social or cultural pressures that may potentially have a divisive influence on a local body of believers? Can you think of some of these things that divide people in the wider society that may be inadvertently carried into the church?

2. Have you seen examples of a local church making a concerted and planned effort to overcome barriers in order to reach into their community or to integrate differing groups into their fellowship (e.g., moving beyond their 'comfort zone', making an effort to communicate in relevant ways, learning language, understanding culture, reaching into the community, etc.)?

3. How much of a balance do you feel the local church should have on "outreach" (ministry to reach unbelievers in their own or other communities) as opposed to "in-church programs" (ministries to the existing church body of believers)? What percentage of church resources - time, personnel, finances, etc. - do you think should be designated to either area? Why?

7.15 Introduction to 'Life'

 OBJECTIVES OF THIS TUTORIAL

This tutorial moves on to a new area of the W.I.L.D. outline: *Life*, and gives an introduction to that area.

Last time
We considered some factors that determine whether a group of God's people will be unified or fragmented. We looked briefly at what Paul told the Galatian and Ephesian churches about how their view of who they are in Christ plays into this…how the old things that once divided them are now irrelevant because of their new identity with Him. We thought about what kind of evidence we'd find in a church that has, or will have, contentions and divisions. We also noted how important it is for believers, right from the beginning, to associate the outward trajectory of the early Church with their own new identity as Jesus' witnesses. And we noted the fact that individuals and groups who are being taught effectively from God's Word will be wrestling with what it means to be relevant witnesses in their immediate circle of acquaintances and that they'll increasingly associate themselves with God's global purposes.

W.I.L.D. highlights important areas to think about
We started out on these Module 7 tutorials by reminding ourselves of the three main metaphors or pictures that God, the Author, has built into reality and used in His Narrative to describe the Church or the Ecclesia of His people: Building, Body and Bride. We know that Jesus Christ is keen for us, like all believers, to participate with Him in His purposes, and so we want to:

— understand how He is building the Church so that whatever we attempt to construct fits with His project,

— share His concern for the Body so that we can contribute effectively to its health, growth and maturity,

— experience something of His love for the Church so we can help to prepare the Bride for His coming.

To do that, we need to engage everything of who He's made us to be - our minds, our wills, our emotions - and to align them with His perspective, intentions and what He's passionate about. This happens as we know Him better through His Narrative - His Word - as we walk in real dependence on Him, as we glean from the experience of others, and as we use the resources, abilities and gifts He provides. The W.I.L.D. framework we're introducing here doesn't replace any of that, but it helps to highlight important areas to keep in mind: as we plan how we can be effectively involved in His work; when we come across proposed methodologies for sharing Truth and church planting; or when we need to assess a situation in which God's Word is already being shared by ourselves or others.

Defining *Life*

So far we've considered five questions for "W" (*Word*) and "I" (*Identity*) respectively. Now we want to move on and do the same with "L" (*Life*). But what exactly are we talking about - what do we mean by *Life* when we use it as one of four lenses through which we consider the impact of Truth on an individual and a group of believers?

Attempts to define life from a semantic (i.e. its meaning as a word) or from a scientific perspective always feel unsatisfactory; they fall far short of the reality. The effort is doomed by the absence of an objective vantage point from which to define something so profound, something so fundamental to…well, to life. And there's something faintly absurd about someone who has been given the gift of life (at least physical life) trying to define it without any reference to the One who is both Life and the Life-giver. Those rather feeble efforts usually try to explain life by contrasting something that's alive, with objects that are dead, or that consist of only inanimate matter. They tend to focus on the processes all living organisms have in common: they react to stimuli, digest, reproduce, and pass their traits on to their offspring, they take in energy, undergo chemical transformation (metabolism), etc. As accurate as these observations may be, they are only descriptions of some of the characteristics of life, not the thing itself. They don't get to the heart, the living soul. They leave us cold because they fall so far short of what we see around us and feel within ourselves. They don't do justice to the dignity and enormous value that we understand God gives to life…when it is the life of His image-bearers, and especially those who have been restored through Christ to a relationship with Himself.

Life as defined in God's Word

So, as we look at the third of our four W.I.L.D. "lenses" to focus on more key aspects of how God works and how we can best contribute, we remind ourselves that any true understanding of what life truly is must begin and end with God. Speaking to the intellectuals in Athens, Paul said about God, that "He Himself gives life and breath to everything" and that "in Him we live and move and exist." (Acts 17:25–28). Certainly in the very succinct Genesis record of God's creation, we glimpse a picture there of vigorous, vibrant, verdant life bursting out everywhere, from single-celled organisms, bacteria, fungi and plants right up to the dazzling complexity of animals. All of this brought into being and energised by the power of God's act of creative communication, His Word. What had been "formless and empty" was now ordered and full of life. The *form* (the universe and the laws that govern it) has *function* (movement, sound, beauty) and *fruit* (the outcomes that God intends).

Adam and Eve

Then, as the climax of creation, He forms a different kind of being, a man, and the first in a race that is to bear God's image. But this shape, lying there, is nothing more than a complex amalgamation of the fundamental elements of creation - electrons, atoms, and minerals that form cells, bones, muscles and organs. Yes, brilliantly constructed, and with amazing potential, but nothing more. That is, until God, in a very direct and personal way transmits - "breathes" the Narrative says - life into this still, cold body. And now *it* becomes *he*: a living, breathing, moving, thinking, speaking, and acting man, a person. The *form* (his physical body) now has *function* (the ability to reason, decide, respond, impact his environment, communicate) and the capacity to produce *fruit* (to hear, relate to, and choose to honor and worship God).

Of course Adam and Eve later chose a different path, the way of death, of separation from the Source of Life. They fell for the great deception - that they could use the gift of life for their own ends, directing it towards outcomes (*fruit*) of their own choosing, without guidance from God, and that the result would be a better, more fulfilling existence. The consequences for them and all their descendants, who also gladly choose the same lie, is a *form* of human life, with some residue of the *function*, but with none of the *fruit* that He intended.

The Children of Israel

We don't have time here to do more than trace the very outline of God's gracious response. How He provided temporary solutions, forms and functions (the sacrifices, the Law, the Tabernacle and Temple, the Levitical priesthood etc.). A provisional connection, accessed by faith, was established between God and man so that, although corrupted by sin, human life could have value and purpose. The life-restoring link was certainly forged between God and individuals, but by choosing the nation of Israel, He also demonstrated the value He places on Him being the energizing force for groups of people who will follow Him. In fact, His commitment was so complete that He came to live among them as a community.

But the constrictive conditions of the Covenant that made His presence possible, also meant that the flow of life was not a free and easy one; it was constrained by elaborate *forms* and repetitive *functions* that were as much about distance and death as they were about access and life. And often the flow was all but blocked by their unfaithfulness. The *forms* were there to remind them of Him, and they legalistically fulfilled the required *functions* of the Law, but without His involvement these became empty religious rituals that didn't produce genuine *fruit*. Eventually He told them He was disgusted and sickened by them endlessly bringing offerings, fasting, burning incense, conducting ceremonies etc. when their lives were so obviously removed from His (Isaiah 1:11–15). He said they had a clear choice "between life and death, between blessings and curses." His heartfelt cry went out to them, "Oh, that you would choose life, so that you and your descendants might live!" (Deuteronomy 30:19). Although during that Old Covenant period there was always a handful of individuals who understood their need for Him as the source of life, the times when the whole nation chose Him as the focus of their corporate existence were rare. The inevitable result was that they were severely hampered in their ability to be a channel of God's life to the other people groups around them as He intended.

The Lord Jesus Christ

The history of God's quest for human beings who'll humbly depend on Him for every aspect of their existence reached a climax with the arrival of His Son on the earth. Here, finally, was someone whose *form* was typically human, but whose every *function* - from an underlying worldview through to values and behavior - were shaped by God's Spirit. He provides us with a model for a life guided by God, but He is far more than that. He is also the avenue for that life. In fact He *is* that life! He asserted this in the clearest terms and, after spending three years with Him, His closest friends and followers on earth had absolutely no doubt that this was true. One of them would later say, "…We saw Him with our own eyes and touched Him with our own hands. He is the Word of life. This one who is life itself was revealed to us, and we have seen Him. And now we testify and proclaim to you that He is the one who is eternal life…" (1 John 1:1,2).

But the life that comes from Him cannot be superimposed on anything else. It's not just a matter of changing forms and functions. That's like trying to load the latest software onto a twenty-year-old computer. It just won't work. Everything has to be replaced - the hardware, the operating system, everything. Using far more powerful and compelling imagery than that, Jesus made this point when He told the Pharisee Nicodemus that for someone to experience the eternal life that Jesus offers, they have to be reborn by an act of His Spirit. This takes place when people believe in Him - in Jesus - and in the death that He would die on their behalf (John 3).

This brings us to something hugely important about His life - the kind that is directly linked to God - it's the opposite of self-focus, self-indulgence and self-protection. In fact, when someone experiences it most fully, they become willing to sacrifice, even to die, to give others access to it. Paul of Tarsus, who'd also been a Pharisee, would later tell a group of believers that they needed the perspective of Christ who willingly gave up the outer form of His existence as God to take on the form of humanity, the role of a slave and the destiny of death (Philippians 2). Jesus Himself said that the love of life for its own sake results in its loss. He used the image of a seed that will sit in a stagnant, lifeless form, with all its potential fruit locked away, unless it is planted and dies in the soil. Only then can it produce what God wants, "a plentiful harvest of new lives" (John 12:24–25).

He, of course, willingly invested His life and, as the rich crop of human lives began to be harvested as a result, it became clear that not only were they individually linked to God, but that He also intended to have a connection to them as a Group. Unlike the basis of the first relationship He'd forged with a people - Israel - this one would not be conditioned by the restrictive forms and functions of the Mosaic Law that spelled death (2 Corinthians 3:6). Because Jesus Himself forms the conduit for this new life, there are no restrictions other than the compelling "Law" of His love and grace. His Spirit coming so dramatically to "indwell" the brand new Ecclesia guaranteed the direct, permanent link to God from the beginning.

God's Word itself

A major part of the Spirit's role in the Church would be to orchestrate the completion of God's revelation, the "word of life" as Paul called it (Philippians 2:16). This would not be, is not, just objective information, OR religious dogma to be manipulated by the powerful, OR text to be interpreted at will, OR a cosy dialogue with the Divine. Having been inspired or "breathed out" by God's Spirit is evocative of Him breathing life into Adam, and by extension, the human race. His Word carries within it His own living, sovereign power (2 Timothy 3:16, Hebrews 4:12). Any attempt we make to define the new life that Jesus has won for us as individuals and a Church has to take into account the role of His Word. It is the scalpel God's Spirit uses to carve away the layers of lifeless *form* and dead *function* that people and cultures hide behind. Exposed, He convinces them that they stand guilty before a righteous, holy Judge (John 16:8). Then, in the receptive conditions of faith, He uses the Word to implant completely new life and nurture it towards health, maturity and productivity (Ephesians 2:5).

This needs to be highlighted because the kind of *Life* we hope to find or want to contribute to - i.e. what we're trying to define in this part of the W.I.L.D. outline - simply doesn't exist without the powerful living impact of God's Word. But as we've also noted, because God has always chosen to involve His faithful people in His purposes, the Spirit does not generally wield this amazingly potent force without their involvement. This ties in with another thread we see woven into His Narrative: although God acts miraculously - and Him producing life through His Word is most definitely a miracle - with only rare and notable exceptions does His activity clearly circumvent the laws He embedded in His Creation. So the supernatural activity of God's Spirit as He brings life through His Word takes place in partnership with His children as they share clearly in the "normal" medium of human language and against the backdrop of people's everyday lives.

Life produces fruit

The same principle holds true for the *fruit* of the life we should be looking for in any situation where Truth is being shared. As we noted before, under the Old Covenant God was not interested in the Jew's religious activity for the sake of it; in fact, it disgusted Him. *Form* and *function* are only legitimate when they produce *fruit*. Using His famous vine analogy, Jesus made it perfectly clear that this *fruit* that is God's intention for His people is only possible when His life is flowing through them (John 15:5). Although still bearing the marks of sin in a world dominated by God's Enemy, their bodies *can* be used as instruments to do what is right for the glory of God (Romans 6:22). This is a miracle that can happen when believers are gathered in a church building together, but it can also happen any day of the week in kitchens, classrooms, offices, factories, tennis courts, village huts, dusty streets and rice fields.

The *fruit* that the Spirit wants to produce in God's people is only possible as they tap into the awesome power of Christ's resurrection, but the results are rarely dramatic and eye-catching. His authentic *fruit* - things like love, kindness and self-control - are usually the result of choices that result in small acts of generosity, the right responses made, tongues being held, encouragement given, the needs of others put first, the courage to speak His name in hostile environments, the discipline to keep moving forward no matter what. These are the true miracles that are the product of Christ's life being lived out. And when these "living sacrifices" are combined, when a group of God's children are gladly offering their minds, arms and legs, their time, creativity and money to Him as a collective act of worship and service in the real world, they add up to much more than the sum of the parts. He is able to use their combined gifts, talents and experiences to produce *fruit* through them as they share His life-giving Word in the local community and beyond.

So as we project what the genuine life of an individual believer or a church should look like, or as we try to recognise it in an existing situation, we need to ask Him for His eyes to see. We need to learn to:

- Picture how appropriate form can serve legitimate function that produces genuine fruit according to His perspective, not according to our own assumptions.
- Detach ourselves from our own formative, cultural church background so when we see form that is familiar to us we don't take that as prima facie evidence that true Life is present (or if we see a different form to assume that true life is not present).
- Look beyond unfamiliar form so that we don't unconsciously assume that it is wrong or, on the other hand, blindly accept its validity just because it looks innovative, exotic or "indigenous".
- Understand how the Spirit uses God's Narrative - His Word - communicated clearly and cohesively, to equip His children in the long-term process of shaping what they do and how they do it according to His purposes.
- Recognise the often small, seemingly unspectacular but authentic fruit of God's Spirit in the lives of individuals and groups of His children, and celebrate them for the miracles they are.

INTRODUCTION TO 'LIFE'

 **DISCUSSION POINTS**

1. Consider each of the points below and discuss the obstacles to each and how they might be overcome.

- Picture how appropriate form can serve legitimate function that produces genuine fruit according to His perspective, not our own assumptions.
- Detach ourselves from our own formative, cultural church background so when we see form that is familiar to us we don't take that as prima facie evidence that true Life is present.
- Look beyond unfamiliar form so that we don't unconsciously assume that it is wrong or, on the other hand, blindly accept its validity just because it looks innovative, exotic or "indigenous".
- Understand how the Spirit uses God's Narrative - His Word - communicated clearly and cohesively, to equip His children in the long-term process of shaping what they do and how they do it according to His purposes.
- Recognise the often small, seemingly unspectacular but authentic fruit of God's Spirit in the lives of individuals and groups of His children, and celebrate them for the miracles they are.

7.16 A relationship with Jesus

> ✓ **OBJECTIVES OF THIS TUTORIAL**
>
> This tutorial looks at the first question in the area of *Life*: 'Are they experiencing a deepening relationship with Jesus, learning to depend more completely on Him in different areas of their lives, and gradually seeing their values and behavior change as a result?'

Last time

We started into the third area of the W.I.L.D. framework, *Life*. We noted the failure of definitions of "life" that don't involve the One who *is* Life and the Life-giver. By contrast, our attempt to encapsulate what Life actually is, focused on God and what He reveals through His Narrative about the life He wants His image bearers to have. We found Him creating plant and animal life, then breathing life into the otherwise inanimate body of Adam. Then, later we saw Him graciously providing a provisional way for fallen humans to still be connected to His Life, with His glorious presence even coming to "dwell" among His Covenant people. But what went before was only preparation, pointing towards the essence of Life, Jesus Christ, who through His death and resurrection created a permanent way for humans to experience authentic life, individually, as local bodies, and as one Church.

Before we consider some specific questions to help us picture and evaluate real life for God's people, there are a few points worth noting:

1. We cannot hope to be exhaustive here. In some ways "life" is a term we use to describe our entire experience of reality, so there's really no end to the issues we could consider. We'll have to be selective and try to pinpoint what will be most helpful.

2. The ability to evaluate, or even to picture, authentic spiritual life depends to a large degree on our own experience of that life. So we need to approach this with real humility, asking God to deepen our own experience and understanding of the life He has given us in Christ.

3. As Paul reminded the Romans (14:10), none of us is in a position to condemn or look down on other believers because each of us will stand before God to have the fruit of our own lives exposed to the light of His scrutiny.

The first question under "L" for *Life*

- <u>Are they experiencing a deepening relationship with Jesus, learning to depend more completely on Him in different areas of their lives, and gradually seeing their values and behavior change as a result?</u>
- Are they gaining clarity about the true purpose for which they exist, and are they increasingly able to identify those things that hinder their life in Christ?
- Are they increasingly able to make good decisions based on their understanding of God's local and global purposes, and to use their time, money and other resources accordingly?
- Are they learning to shape the *form* of what they do to serve whatever *function* they are convinced will lead to the *fulfillment* of God's objectives?
- Are they growing in their commitment to reproducing the life they have in Christ, are they equipped with the resources and skills to do so, and are they prioritizing opportunities where there is real need and hunger?

A deepening relationship with Jesus

So what does a *deepening relationship with Jesus* look like and what are the results, the fruit? Paul talks to the Ephesian church about Christ making His home in their hearts (Ephesians 3:17). The result of this warm companionship, he said a few lines later, is an experience of "all the fullness of life and power that comes from God." (Ephesians 3:19). Elsewhere he encourages the Colossians to let their "roots grow down into Him [Jesus]" (Colossians 2:7). As for outcomes, he says that their faith will grow strong in the truth and they'll overflow with thankfulness. Further on he describes some tangible fruit that will result if they'll allow Christ's rich teaching to become a significant part of their life as a church: they will have the wisdom to teach and encourage each other, and their gratitude will result in heartfelt communal praise to God (Colossians 3:16). Writing to friends in Philippi, he reflects on his own relationship with Christ and how life really has become all about Him. In fact, he has come to know and love his Saviour so much that if there's no work left for him on earth, he's more than happy to die and go to be with Jesus (Philippians 1:21). In this same letter he hard-wires knowing Christ with an experience of "the mighty power that raised him from the dead" (Philippians 3:10).

From these few samples and the whole of God's Narrative, we can summarize just some of the results we should expect to see from a "deepening relationship with Jesus":

- A sense of purpose and completeness rather than futility and emptiness.
- An inner strength and calm that is different from self-assertiveness and false optimism.
- A stability that is not at all the same as inflexibility.
- An understanding of Truth that is authentic and not just theory or knowledge.
- The ability to help others - through words and actions - to know Jesus more deeply.
- A sense of gratitude and thankfulness rather than a sense of entitlement.
- A readiness to praise God as a response to His revelation of Himself.
- A sense of hope about an eternity with Jesus rather than fear of the future or a preoccupation with the physical reality of this world.

Learning to depend on Him

Along with *a deepening relationship with Jesus*, this first question (under "L" for *Life*) also poses: *learning to depend more completely on Him in different areas of their lives* as a hallmark of real spiritual life. The consequence of not depending on Him is also true. Human existence since the Fall has been defined by our ancestors' choice *not* to live in dependence on the Creator, and the default of every human heart since has been *away* from reliance on God. That initial choice opened the door for death and innumerable smaller choices since have allowed it to dominate over life (Romans 5:12).

It's impossible to overstate just how thoroughly conditioned people are to depend on something or someone other than God. Individual worldviews and the societies that give them a communal expression are elaborate structures that help people avoid any sense of need in their lives for the true God. Created originally to be dependent on Him, people instead turn to other lesser "gods", or to each other, to ideas, cultural narratives, religious practices or physical things; and most of all, to themselves. If their cultural traditions include a knowledge of the true God and any sense of His righteous claims, their self-dependence "DNA" will always compel them to look for ways to appease and approach Him through their own efforts. This also holds true when people are exposed to His Narrative for the first time. But when it is communicated clearly, He uses His Word to demonstrate the futility of those efforts, leading them to put their complete dependence - their faith - in Christ. As a result, He turns off their bogus life-support system that has kept them reliant on everything other than God, and the line on the screen goes flat - they die. They've been "crucified with Christ", as Paul so vividly described it to the Galatians. Their new lives, by complete contrast, are then *ontologically* (i.e. in their very being) hooked up to His eternal life, designed and recreated now for complete dependence on Him (Galatians 2:20 and 6:15).

The problem, of course, is that old habits die hard. Even with God's life coursing through their spiritual veins, the "muscle memory" imprinted by years of not relying on God still causes them to compulsively find their security elsewhere. Some of the more obvious dependencies are recognized, even by the wider society, as unhealthy addictions. Others, often related to sexuality, are not even viewed as harmful obsessions by many cultures, but just as a matter of personal choice. In some instances people are miraculously freed from these enslavements at salvation, but often they need very specific and long-term help that allows them to truly deal with their addictions in light of their new life in Christ. But even though these dependencies might be the easiest to recognise and have the most visibly devastating results, in essence they share a great deal in common with the life-long challenge all believers face: learning to trust God completely for every aspect of their lives.

How deeply God's Truth has impacted someone's life, and how far they've come in their journey towards true dependence on Him, is often most visible in times of crisis or change. We can observe how they deal with upheaval, with sickness, danger, loss, financial difficulties. Also when they are dealing with hurt and disappointment in relationships or facing unjust criticism. How do they handle a major decision or cope with sudden life changes? Where do they turn in these situations? Is it gradually becoming a habit of life to turn to God as their ultimate security, comfort, friend and guide? Not with demands that He makes them or their children healthy; or with a false hope that He will ensure their financial prosperity; or the assumption that He will fix every relationship problem; but in the quiet confidence that no matter what the circumstances, He will do what's best for them and others as He pursues His just, gracious purposes in the world. Obviously growth and maturity in these areas is *not* about a fake silver-lining optimism and denial of the realities that are part of living and dying in a fallen world. There is always a battle, a need for every believer to constantly remind themselves of God's promises, to discipline their minds and wills to actively depend on Him. Maturity comes by habitual "use" or "through training", as the writer of Hebrews puts it, (Hebrews 5:14) and it's evidence of this that we should be looking for.

Dependence on God in the life of a church

Clearly, we've barely scratched the surface of what *dependence on God* looks like in someone's life, but before we move on we need to briefly make some observations about how this plays out in the corporate life of a church. Just as for individuals, how much a body of believers is depending on God for their life together often shows itself most clearly in challenging circumstances; when an influential leader leaves, when there's external threat, when finances for church programs are tight, when numbers are in decline. But there are also other indicators. For example, we can ask ourselves:

- Is there a confidence in God's Spirit speaking through the lives of members and His Word as the *primary* way He attracts and integrates people into the life of the church...or is the *focus* on personalities, entertainment, marketing and creating a pleasurable experience for anyone who might come along?
- Is the tone of the prayers and testimonies of the church body one of gratitude and praise for all God has provided spiritually as well as physically, and a recognition that He is sufficient for all needs...or is there a sense of entitlement and a preoccupation with Him meeting their earthly expectations?
- Is there a willingness to interact with other believers who hold different perspectives, and engage in authentic ways with the majority culture...or is there a feeling of being under siege and a reluctance to believe that God can keep them from error and help them to be truly *in* the world without being defined *by* it?
- Is there a sense of vision, of facing challenges together in God's strength, of taking up opportunities...or is there a dominant voice of caution, of preserving the status quo, an unwillingness to use resources without ironclad guarantees that they'll be replenished?

Changing values and behavior

The other point this first question (under "L" for *Life*) makes, is that if God's Word is being effectively shared with an individual or group, we will be *gradually seeing their values and behavior change as a result*. The order here is of critical importance. If we are imagining teaching God's Word in a church planting context, for example, part of our mental picture will almost definitely include people moving away from destructive behavior after conversion so they can live in ways that are pleasing to Him. Or, if we are already involved in sharing Truth and discipling others, then very naturally we'll be eagerly looking for signs of change to indicate that our partnership with God's Spirit is bearing fruit. We're right to think that way, but the challenge, as we noted in Tutorial 7.8, when we were discussing how the *authority* of God's Word plays out, is that there are all kinds of motivations for behavioral change. In our quest to work effectively alongside Him in His purposes for His children and His church, we don't want to be part of forcing people to change or even providing them with the wrong motivation. We want to be able to encourage and celebrate authentic spiritual growth and not to "enable" the old addiction of self-dependency by advocating change that's the product of anything other than Christ's own life.

And so, as we noted, the order in which the change takes place is critical: first people's values are changed by God's Word, then their behavior will follow suit. Paul explained to the believers in Rome that God would transform them into new people by changing the way they thought (Romans 12:2), or as he put it to the Colossian church, Christians can live in ways that are consistent with their new natures as they get to know their Creator and become like Him (Colossians 3:10). Peter described it yet another way: as God's children learn to depend on what He promises, they can share in His own character and be free of the corrupting influence of their own desires (2 Peter 1:4).

Of course it's tough enough to accurately evaluate our own motivation, much less someone else's. But with God's help in avoiding harsh judgment, we should be able to discern something of what is real and what is not. For example, it's troubling when we see a new believer suddenly assume the look and mannerisms of "Christianity", when they are obviously trying to live up to an external set of expectations. It should also raise red flags when we see behavioral change in someone who we know has not yet had sufficient teaching or discipleship for that change to be based on. Or when we know they have been exposed to a perspective of God and His Word that puts them under condemnation and implies that they can somehow please God through their own efforts to improve. On the positive side, we can be reassured when we hear an individual or group of believers speaking of God's grace in their lives, when they have been taught about who they are in Christ and we begin to see small choices made in His strength that are gradually becoming habitual.

Some extra questions

To go along with the first question in the area of *Life*, 'Are they experiencing a deepening relationship with Jesus, learning to depend more completely on Him in different areas of their lives, and gradually seeing their values and behavior change as a result?', we can also ask:

- Is their relationship with Jesus producing thankfulness, stability, authenticity, a willingness to serve others, and confidence about eternity?
- Are they able to identify old habits of dependency that get in the way of completely relying on Christ for their standing in God's eyes and for all their true needs?
- Is the direction of their lives gradually changing, not through their own efforts to try to be "Christian", but as the Spirit teaches and equips them to live out the attitudes of Christ in valid ways?

? **DISCUSSION POINTS**

1. Is the question of whether your own relationship with Jesus is continuing to deepen something you ask yourself regularly? <u>If not</u>, why? Do you have a reason (e.g. you don't think it's possible to know, or the idea of evaluating spiritual life has some bad connotations from your past, etc.)? OR, is it just not something that you've thought about much? <u>If so</u>, (1) How do you tend to gauge it? (2) Do you feel your ways of measuring are valid?

2. Do you think that someone with an addiction or a diagnosed psychological condition like depression should be freed from that at salvation? Please explain your answer. If you don't think so, in broad terms describe the kind of help that a new believer wrestling with an issue like that needs. Would you recommend them getting clinical therapy or only Christian counselling? What part should church leaders/shepherds have in a situation like that?

3. As you're getting to know a young believer, what kinds of things might cause you to wonder if they are falling into the trap of trying to conform to a set of standards they associate with being a "Christian"? Given the opportunity, how would you try to help them?

7.17 The purpose for which we exist

 OBJECTIVES OF THIS TUTORIAL

This tutorial looks at the second and third questions under the area of *Life*: 'Are they gaining clarity about the true purpose for which they exist, and are they increasingly able to identify those things that hinder their life in Christ?' and 'Are they increasingly able to make good decisions based on their understanding of God's local and global purposes, and to use their time, money and other resources accordingly?'

Last time

We asked ourselves just what a deepening relationship with Jesus looks like and noted some things that the New Testament says about this. We concluded that we'd see things like: a sense of purpose, inner strength, stability, authentic understanding of Truth, ability to help others know Jesus more, thankfulness and a sense of hope in eternity.

We also talked about how the ingrained habits of *self* and *other* dependence don't automatically stop when someone is born again. Believers need to learn and practice the reality that in Christ they have died and risen again, newly created, specially designed for a life of trusting Him.

Finally, we reminded ourselves that valid change in behavior for believers doesn't come from their own effort, but as the Spirit uses Truth to change their thinking and values.

The second question under "L" for *Life*

- Are they experiencing a deepening relationship with Jesus, learning to depend more completely on Him in different areas of their lives, and gradually seeing their values and behavior change as a result?

- <u>Are they gaining clarity about the true purpose for which they exist, and are they increasingly able to identify those things that hinder their life in Christ?</u>

- Are they increasingly able to make good decisions based on their understanding of God's local and global purposes, and to use their time, money and other resources accordingly?

THE PURPOSE FOR WHICH WE EXIST

- Are they learning to shape the *form* of what they do to serve whatever *function* they are convinced will lead to the *fulfillment* of God's objectives?
- Are they growing in their commitment to reproducing the life they have in Christ, are they equipped with the resources and skills to do so, and are they prioritizing opportunities where there is real need and hunger?

Back in Tutorial 7.12, as we considered the second question under "I" for Identity, we noted how closely interwoven *identity* and *purpose* are. Who someone believes they are plays out in what they assume their lives are all about. We can state it another way: what people do, what is valuable to them, how they spend their time and energy…these things say a great deal about how they see themselves in their spiritual, physical and relational "world". Also whether they see themselves only as inhabitants of this finite, temporal universe or of something larger, transcendent, and continuing, even eternal.

To help us think this through, let's imagine the different responses we'd get if we asked people under various worldview labels the question, "Why do you exist?" (We should acknowledge that the labels might not be the ones some of the people themselves would use or be comfortable with.)

An *individualist* might say something like: "I exist to be successful - as I define 'success' - to express and to please myself."

A *Muslim*: "I exist by the will of Allah, to serve him."

A *relativist*: "To be free of intolerance and to celebrate diversity."

A *tantric Buddhist*: "The question is meaningless and unhelpful."

A *scientific naturalist*: "I exist as the result of chance and natural laws in a closed system."

An *animist*: "To maintain harmony between the living and dead, the physical and spiritual worlds."

A *consumerist*: "To get everything I want, to be comfortable and to be entertained."

A *New Ageist*: "To find the God within and to be fulfilled."

Someone who sees themselves as a *victim*: "To find healing and freedom from pain."

A *Vedic Hindu*: "I, if there is even an 'I', exist to find self-realization through becoming one with Brahman, the Universal Being."

Admittedly this was not a real survey - we cheated by setting it up ourselves - but it should serve to point out that when someone is asked the question, "Why do you exist?" their pre-existing worldview forms the ground from which they reply. The fact that many people never consider the question at all might represent intellectual laziness, but it's often just as much the result of a subconscious worldview commitment *not* to wrestle with all the implications of existence. Also, it's worth noting that the worldview of most of our fictional respondents shaped not only how they answered, but also how they understood the question itself. Most, if not all, were actually responding to, "What or who has caused you to exist?" or, "What do you do with your existence?" Those are obviously valid questions, but they are derivatives of the primary issue - the real reason we exist.

Why do we exist?

We know that the true ground for answering the question of why we exist lies "outside" (i.e. in time, space and scope) of our finite lives, in the primary existence of the Three-In-One relational, communicating God. It's our Creator's glorious, gracious and righteous purposes flowing from who He is, that give meaning to human existence. And for us as re-born children of God, the "why" of our existence can only accurately be answered against the backdrop of Golgotha and Gethsemane. Christ's sacrifice and victory, along with His Spirit's presence, is also the basis for the Church's existence.

Okay, so those are existential truths that no believer or church would argue with. But as a measure of how effectively Truth is impacting a context, our second question here under "L" for "*Life*" is meant to help us picture something more than just theoretical or doctrinal statements, the kind of points that are made in a sermon. They cannot remain as truths or beliefs held in some conceptual category but have to play out in real life. "Why do I exist?" or "Why do we exist as a church?" is a question that should be asked and answered in the normal course of events on a regular basis. And from there, spin-off questions, "So why in this particular place and time?" "Why particularly *us*?" and, "Are we actually fulfilling the purpose He has us here for?" Whether or not an individual or church wrestles with those kinds of questions on a regular basis is itself an indicator of maturity.

And how would we hope to see those questions being answered? Well, first of all, it would be enormously encouraging to hear the answers framed by God's *Word*; by a sense of their place within His redemptive Narrative - past, present and future. "God has made it very clear to us through His Word why we're here. He has a specific purpose for us, just as He did for the Israelite nation, just as He did for the early believers in Jerusalem, and then the churches in Ephesus, Rome and elsewhere. We're here as a continuation of what Jesus initiated and then passed on to the apostles." Secondly, it would be a very positive sign if responses to those questions also included mentions of *Identity*, "We're ordinary, needy people through whom God chooses to demonstrate His grace. We exist here as worshippers of God. We understand that we're here to reflect His light in the darkness." Thirdly, we'd be heartened if there were references to the whole area of *Discipleship*, "We exist here because our Master placed us here at this time in history. We exist as His disciples to bring others into the same relationship with Him. Our purpose is to follow Him and represent Him in this community and out into the world that He loves."

What would represent a further level of maturity is if they are (as our second question under "L" for *Life* puts it) "increasingly able to identify those things that hinder their life in Christ." It's certainly wonderful if an individual or group of believers can describe with real clarity the reasons they exist in the ways we've just imagined. But an equally vital next step is being able to self-evaluate - with the Holy Spirit's help - and identify those areas that represent the greatest challenges and obstacles to them actually doing what God has made them for. Sometimes it might simply be more teaching and equipping that is needed. Or it might just be that more time, patience and growth is required. Of course it's always accurate to say that more faith, greater dependence on God and deeper certainty about His promises is needed. Often, as we've discussed previously, the greatest challenges are represented by habits of life that have been brought over into the new life in Christ. And then there's the whole range of obstacles presented by the values of the surrounding culture. Maybe the wrong people are having too much influence, or there's a culture of gossip, rebellious attitudes, or personality conflicts on the leadership team. In truth, the list of things that can hinder an individual or group of believers' life in Christ is endless. But the point is that the ability for an individual or group of believers to self-assess and identify where their greatest obstacles lie, what might be tripping them up, what areas need attention, what is distracting them...the willingness and ability to do this is a real hallmark of maturity.

Some extra questions

To go along with the second question under *Life*, 'Are they gaining clarity about the true purpose for which they exist, and are they increasingly able to identify those things that hinder their life in Christ?', we can also ask:

- Do they have a growing desire to understand why God has placed them in their particular place and time?
- Is their perspective of why they exist being shaped by God's Word, His view of their Identity, and by the Discipleship relationship they have with Jesus Christ?

- Are they learning to evaluate, with God's help, how well they are fitting into the purposes God has for them, the immediate challenges they face, and the areas that need to be adjusted to fulfill those purposes?

The third question under "L" for *Life*

- Are they experiencing a deepening relationship with Jesus, learning to depend more completely on Him in different areas of their lives, and gradually seeing their values and behavior change as a result?
- Are they gaining clarity about the true purpose for which they exist, and are they increasingly able to identify those things that hinder their life in Christ?
- <u>Are they increasingly able to make good decisions based on their understanding of God's local and global purposes, and to use their time, money and other resources accordingly?</u>
- Are they learning to shape the outward form of what they do, to genuinely reflect the inner reality of the life they have in Christ?
- Are they growing in their commitment to reproducing the life they have in Christ, are they equipped with the resources and skills to do so, and are they prioritizing opportunities where there is real need and hunger?

The previous question under "L" for *Life* considered how clear an individual or group of believers might be about why they exist. We did touch on some practical indicators but on the whole it was a theoretical understanding we reflected on. But in this, the third question, we want to focus on some of the more tangible results in the lives of God's people as they glimpse the scope of His purposes and the part He invites them to play.

Making good decisions

Growing maturity never involves a decrease in the dilemmas or difficult decisions believers face. But the longer they walk with the Lord the deeper marked, and the more easily followed, are the tracks they use to seek His will and come to appropriate conclusions. As we picture the effective impact of God's Word, or if we're in a situation where we need to evaluate what's already happening, the way people go about making decisions presents a vital sign of health and growth.

We know this from the rest of life. One of the features of adolescence is apparently haphazard decision making. A mantra of many parents of teenagers is, "What were you thinking? Or weren't you thinking at all?" The specific instance they're being roasted for (or, depending on who's telling the story, receiving "constructive input" about) - e.g.

how they spent their money, where they chose to go, who they were hanging out with, why they put something off - is being held up as evidence of them not thinking. Of course they *might* have thought briefly, but what's questionable is how careful and valid their thought processes were. They're being charged with choosing selfishly, prioritizing wants over real needs, valuing immediate gratification over long-term gain, or being influenced by peer pressure over family values. They started life, like all infants, by responding to the world around them in ways that were completely spontaneous, instinctive and related to immediate necessities. Now into their second decade, their world has expanded, but according to their parents they are still making some random, selfish and ill-advised choices. Their perspective needs to grow so they make decisions based on realities beyond themselves, the present, the immediate, the opinions of whoever they happen to be with. In fact, we can say that the process of becoming more mature is learning to make decisions on an increasingly wider and more solid basis than is currently the case.

For believers and the churches they are part of, this widening perspective, in the words of this third question under *Life*, is "an understanding of God's local and global purposes". The *understanding* we're picturing here isn't theoretical but a real-life, real world, rubber meets the road, embracing of those purposes in mind, heart, and will. It's the map on which they habitually locate themselves and navigate by. It most certainly involves overwhelming gratitude for His intentions for them personally, but in their expanding view they see themselves in their setting as people who benefit from His grace so they can share it with others. Like Paul of Tarsus and his companions, they are grasping the fact that God has shone His light into their hearts not only so they can feel its warmth and comfort but so that others will be drawn to Him, the Light of the world, as well. And that realization begins to actually shape the way they make big and small decisions.

In the passage (2 Corinthians 4) where the apostle uses his famous "clay pots" metaphor, it's in the context of him reflecting on what motivates his church planting and nurturing team to share God's Word. They don't believe God has shone His light into their hearts just for their own benefit. It's also about Him using them, in all their weak humanity, to shine His light out to others. And that perspective has been costly in some very real, tangible ways. It has meant them giving up what feels familiar, comfortable and secure to go through experiences that are unsettling, painful and very dangerous. But they are making their decisions in light of something infinitely bigger and richer than what is right in front of them here and now. By faith they're seeing the message of God's grace going out to one community after another until the job is done. And they look forward to a day when they're standing among all believers, including their friends from Corinth, before God's throne enjoying His presence with them.

As we look for evidence of the impact of God's Word in the choices of individuals or the corporate decision-making of a group, it's not always going to show itself in dramatic, watershed changes of direction. A much more likely, and in the end probably a more healthy, picture is gradual progress with some missteps and poor decisions showing up here and there. But what we hope to see is people increasingly bringing an awareness of God's purposes and the part He might have for them into the frame as they determine priorities, allocate resources and choose directions.

Some extra questions

To go along with the third question under *Life*, 'Are they increasingly able to make good decisions based on their understanding of God's local and global purposes, and to use their time, money and other resources accordingly?', we can also ask:

- Are they learning to recognize how personal and cultural preferences can exert a subtle but powerful influence on the directions their choices take them?
- Does their decision making process involve them regularly asking God how He wants to involve them in the things He's doing in their immediate vicinity and beyond?
- Is their relationship with Jesus and growing familiarity with His perspectives having an observable impact on major life-changing decisions as well as everyday priorities and choices?

The following two stories are fictional, but the circumstances are real:

Jiao and Feng

My name is Jiao, and my husband is Feng. We come from a large industrial city in north-eastern China. We both graduated from university and Feng's economics degree prepared him to oversee the finances at his father's ceramics factory. I gave up my career in advertising after the birth of our son, Liang. We became believers before we were married through the outreach of a house church and have been active members since.

Some months ago Feng ran into a former classmate that he'd lost touch with, but who was back home for Spring Festival. Later, over lunch at our favorite dumpling restaurant near the river, he told us that he's living down in Sichuan province, working among minority people there. Up 'til now, I guess we'd assumed that pretty much everyone in China can speak Mandarin and so could hear the Gospel if they wanted to. But since talking with that guy we haven't been able to get it out of our minds...to think that millions of people in our own country are cut off from the Truth.

In fact, we've started talking with the leaders at our fellowship about the possibility of moving to the south-west to work with Feng's friend. They were cautiously encouraging, but it was a totally different story when we mentioned the idea to our parents. Wow! We probably should have known the reaction we'd get. At first they refused to believe it, then they got angry. My mother wouldn't talk to me for days. And it has been tense with Feng's dad at the factory. They've said things like, "How could you even think about taking our only grandson away from us? It's barbaric down there, not even civilised. You'd waste the education we paid for. You'll die there, and then who will look after us in our old age? You don't love us." On and on! We don't like to upset them but what can we do? And actually, there is some truth in what they say. There are some real difficulties we'd face in terms of educating our son in an undeveloped region like that. And then of course there is the reality of paying the bills, and health insurance...so many challenges.

But then we look at the pictures our friend has been posting on Qzone (like FaceBook) of minority people in the mountains with their traditional dress. And we remember his description of how much they need to hear about Jesus, and the changes he's seen among the few he's been able to share the Gospel with now he knows their language. We're asking God what to do. Should we take the safe, secure route that is expected of us by our family and friends? Or are God's plans for the world more important?

....

Glasgow Church Plant

Our combined leadership team meeting this morning was pretty intense. Three of us were the first ones who moved with our families eight years ago to plant a church in this rather depressed area of Glasgow, largest city in Scotland. At the beginning it was just us and two single mothers from the council estate, what we call a *housing scheme*. We met in a living room, but we quickly outgrew that and had to rent a room behind a travel agent's office. God blessed by bringing new people to faith, and we had to move again. We've been in our current spot for nearly four years. It was a filthy old building, formerly a print shop that we were able to buy for next to nothing and clean up after we got rid of the machines.

Actually, the building featured in today's discussion. The thing is, even though it has more than enough room, it's less than ideal in a number of ways. It's tucked away down the end of an alley in an industrial area. It would take a lot of money to make the outside look presentable. And it is cold and draughty in winter, pretty expensive to heat.

So there's a push from some on the church staff to move again. They feel in this location we're only appealing to a particular segment of the society. And there's some truth to that. Our church body certainly has a high proportion of underprivileged and new migrants. There are not all that many stable families represented. The advocates for moving want to buy a property and develop a purpose-built facility in a better suburb a few miles away so that we can appeal to a wider range of people and so we'll be able to be a more visible presence in a community.

But some of us have serious concerns. We feel a move to that area could alienate some of those who have been part of the church for years. They might not feel comfortable in that kind of setting. And we tend to believe that the church gathering is not really the place for evangelism. But without doubt the biggest issue is money. A move and building project would mean going into debt and tying up most of our funds for the next ten years. It would curtail some of the community welfare projects we're currently involved in. And, on paper at least, we wouldn't be able to financially support two of our families who've been talking about getting involved in a ministry to asylum seekers in Edinburgh, or a single guy who wants to get training to work in Africa.

Neither side doubts the other's sincerity, but we definitely see things differently. We all want to please the Lord and see His kingdom expanded, but how can we determine which way to go?

THE PURPOSE FOR WHICH WE EXIST

❓ DISCUSSION POINTS

1. Imagine, after being in China for three years studying Mandarin, you meet Jiao and Feng at their fellowship. Over lunch at their favorite dumpling stall they explain their dilemma and ask for your counsel as a foreign believer. What would you say to them?

2. If you were part of the leadership team from the church plant in Glasgow, which side of the debate do you think you'd support - staying in the current premises or moving? What reasons would you give?

➡ ACTIVITIES

1. Imagine that the leadership team from that church in Glasgow has invited you, as an objective facilitator, to help them move beyond the deadlock they find themselves in. What truths and principles would you remind them about? What steps would you suggest they follow in coming to the right decision?

7.18 Form, function, fulfilment

> ✓ **OBJECTIVES OF THIS TUTORIAL**
>
> This tutorial looks at the fourth and fifth questions under the area of *Life*: 'Are they learning to shape the form of what they do to serve whatever function they are convinced will lead to the fulfilment of God's objectives?' and 'Are they growing in their commitment to reproducing the life they have in Christ, are they equipped with the resources and skills to do so, and are they prioritizing opportunities where there is real need and hunger?'

Last time

We considered how maturity for an individual or group of believers is marked by a growing clarity about why they exist in their particular place and time. We noted that it would be a very positive sign to hear them describe the reasons for their existence in terms of being part of God's Narrative, made to be His worshippers and servants, and now disciples of Jesus. Also to observe them accurately pinpointing areas that get in the way of them fulfilling God's purposes for them.

Following on from this, we thought about how maturity also results in people learning to make decisions on an increasingly broader basis, and how this is a gradual process of choosing to live more and more in light of God's purposes for their immediate context and for the world.

The fourth question under "L" for *Life*

- Are they experiencing a deepening relationship with Jesus, learning to depend more completely on Him in different areas of their lives, and gradually seeing their values and behavior change as a result?
- Are they gaining clarity about the true purpose for which they exist, and are they increasingly able to identify those things that hinder their life in Christ?
- Are they increasingly able to make good decisions based on their understanding of God's local and global purposes, and to use their time, money and other resources accordingly?

- Are they learning to shape the *form* of what they do to serve whatever *function* they are convinced will lead to the *fulfilment* of God's objectives?
- Are they growing in their commitment to reproducing the life they have in Christ, are they equipped with the resources and skills to do so, and are they prioritizing opportunities where there is real need and hunger?

Form and function

Form - the shape and structure of something; the particular mode, appearance, etc., in which a thing or person manifests itself; behavior according to a fixed or accepted standard.

Function - the natural action or intended purpose of a person or thing in a specific role; to operate or perform as specified; to work properly.

Fulfillment - to bring into actuality; to carry something out satisfactorily; to bring something to completion.

In an 1896 article architect Louis Sullivan wrote: "It is the pervading law of all things organic and inorganic, of all things physical and metaphysical, of all things human and all things superhuman, of all true manifestations of the head, of the heart, of the soul, that the life is recognizable in its expression, that form ever follows function. This is the law." (Underlining added). It's likely that Sullivan was being ironic because his own architecture was actually quite decorative and not just functional. But his statement became something of a credo for the *Functionalism* that would impact architecture for the first half of the twentieth century.

The idea was that whatever a building is meant to be used for - its intended function(s) - should be the only consideration in design. Decisions about *form* - size, configuration, shape, even decorative style - should only serve this *function*. It fitted well with *Marxism* and can be seen exemplified in some of the rather grim buildings and monuments of Stalinist Russia and Maoist China. It also went along with *Modernism* and the assumption that science would eventually describe all of nature in formulas which technology could then use to fix all the woes of society. And of course all of this intertwined with *Darwinian* theories of evolution and a materialistic view of life that attempted to replace the Truth of a personal Designer and Creator with an entirely mechanistic model in which *form* had no purpose other than the survival *functions* of the species.

To be ridiculous for a moment, imagine what a Creator, influenced by twentieth century *functionalism*, would design if He decided there was a need for something that would produce fruit, give shade, provide a place for birds to nest, and could be sawn up for timber. You'll agree that the result would be something with far less color, variety, and beauty than what we call "trees" in English. Or imagine how different it would be to snorkel on a coral reef or look at a sunset in such a universe. At the other end of the spectrum, and no less absurd, would be a God who took the approach of the so-called *postmodern* architect Peter Eisenman who famously said, "I don't do function." What a chaotic and ultimately unliveable place the universe would be! Thankfully, we know from what God has revealed of Himself through His Narrative and through nature, that He seamlessly blends *form* and *function*. The Great Architect, who put into place the laws that make the universe work, is also the Great Artist who created beautiful things, and gave us the capacity to appreciate beauty.

Form and function in the Church

We can see this too in the way He is building His Church. As we've noted elsewhere in these tutorials, He is going about His great building project carefully and purposefully, but clearly He's not aiming for drab, industrial uniformity. In Ephesians 3:10, Paul says that in this age it's through the Church that God has chosen to "display his wisdom in its rich variety". Elsewhere the apostle stressed just how many different kinds of opportunities the Lord has given us to serve Him and each other because, he said, God "works in different ways" (1 Corinthians 12:6). A little later in the same chapter he makes the point that, just like the human body, the Church is made up of a dazzling assortment of parts that are all designed to fulfil the function God intends. Likewise, Peter tells the churches he's writing to that God has given them gifts "from his great variety of spiritual gifts" (1 Peter 4:10). And if there's any doubt at all about God's delight in diversity, they are answered by John's prophetic vision of the completed Church - a vast crowd made up of every ethnic group standing before the throne of the Lamb (Revelation 7:9).

So there's this rich variety and diversity in the kinds of people that make up the Church, in the work that it has been given and in the skills and gifts needed to do that work… in other words, in both *form* and *function*. But God is seamlessly blending all of that together so that the final result - the *fulfilment* - will be exactly as He intends. This pattern should inform the way individual believers and churches decide what to do and how to do it. And it should also be clearly in our minds when we are picturing sharing God's Word in a cross-cultural situation or if we are considering a proposed church planting strategy, or if we find ourselves in a position of evaluating how effectively Truth is impacting a context different from what's most familiar to us.

Part of a believer's growth towards maturity is learning to emotionally and consciously detach themselves from the *forms* they've grown up with: to identify and discard assumptions that things have to look and sound a certain way, to occur at a set time or in a particular place, to have a particular style and to follow a certain order. In the setting of the church, those assumptions can be particularly deep-seated. The tendency is to confuse aspects of the setting in which Truth had a formative impact, with the Truth itself. Elevating *form* over *function* without *fulfilment* clearly in view leads to legalism, syncretism or, most often, a combination of the two. Of course a knee-jerk rejection of familiar *forms* just because they are familiar does not go along with maturity, in fact quite the opposite. Likewise, an attempt to discard *form* altogether, as some have done, is unhealthy and futile - even chaos is a kind of form.

Principles from God's Word

Thankfully God hasn't left His children or His Church alone to decide what *fulfilment* (i.e. final goals) He is moving them towards, the *functions* to engage in, or even the most appropriate *forms* to adopt. He has provided His Word that states His intentions and demonstrates them through His actions in the Narrative. From the Old Testament, we can learn the *functions* God intended for His people then, and find very detailed descriptions of the *forms* that He knew would best serve those. Accurately viewed through the lens of Him revealing Himself and preparing for the Messiah's arrival in that historic, covenantal and cultural setting, believers today can glean guiding principles - that will emerge more fully under the New Covenant - and apply them directly to what they are doing and how they are going about it.

Jesus' life and teachings contain a wealth of instruction with direct application for believers and churches in any time or place. The perspective that led Him to willingly exchange the "form of God" for the "form of a servant" (in the terms the 17th century translators chose for Philippians 2:6-7) is foundational to any clarity and maturity His followers might reach about these issues. Also, from Jesus' polemic against the empty legalism of the Jews and its leading practitioners, the *Scribes and Pharisees*, there are incredibly valuable lessons to be learned about what God *doesn't* want. They were like tombs, He said, that hide internal decay with neat, presentable exteriors: like trees that produce foliage but no useful fruit; they were obsessed with religious activity but had no relationship with God. And of course there is endless scope for considering the spiritual and practical implications in Jesus' resurrection, and what it means - as the apostles would later explicate - to still bear the outward *forms* of sin and death while having the capacity to *function* on the basis of Christ's new life within.

But it's the Acts Narrative, with explication from the apostles' more propositional teaching in the epistles that provides God's people with the most directly applicable pattern for determining how to function. Here can be found those parts of the account God wanted told about the first groups of New Covenant believers being guided by God's Spirit as they began to decide things like; how, when and where to meet together;

how to give and share what they've been blessed with; how the spiritual leading and more practical administration of the church should take place; how to pray and worship God together; how to obey Christ's specific commands to baptize new converts and to use simple symbols of food and drink to remember His sacrifice; what to wear and how to greet each other; how to disciple others and encourage the next generation of leaders; how to witness for Him and see new outposts of His Church established; how practically to function under the headship of Christ while also valuing interdependence and the help that comes through fellowship with other bodies of believers.

Significantly, under the New Covenant, the exact *form* that the *function* took is not given in detail or laid out as bullet-point directives. There's clear evidence too that there was freedom given by the Spirit for the specifics of how things should be done to flex and morph with the context and circumstances as the Church reached out to new areas. We're reminded of the principle we've already noted: God loves to blend diversity of *form* with effective *function* in the *fulfilment* of His overall purposes.

Forms based on purpose

Through God's Word, we understand that these are some of the most significant purposes God has given to local churches: providing a safe, caring environment for members; giving access to encouragement, instruction and correction from God's Word; facilitating worship, fellowship and obedience to specific commands and general principles; helping members to function in their God given gifts through discipleship and equipping; contributing to the outward thrust of the global Church into needy communities, nearby and distant. One measure of maturity for churches then, is how well they already have, or are developing, a process for articulating those purposes and determining how to do things in ways that best serve those purposes in light of their own unique dynamics and context.

Most new churches go through an initial period of establishing *forms*, but it is often surprising how quickly these can become entombed in tradition. Cross-cultural church planters have to take great care that they are not inadvertently imposing their own cultural preferences (or even their disillusionment with certain *forms* that may not be inappropriate) on the new group. Churches, new or old, that exist within a denominational structure, or who identify with a particular ecclesiological stream, face unique challenges when it comes to feeling the freedom to regularly evaluate and adjust *forms*. Generational change, a general drift away from Biblical "proficiency" (especially in the West), shifting demographics, trends in worship styles (particularly in today's connected world), new technologies, and changes in the larger community…these are just some of the factors that churches have to wrestle with as they seek to function in relevant, authentic and appropriate ways.

As we project into the future or observe an existing context, we would be confident of a church moving towards maturity in terms of *form*, *function* and *fulfilment* if it was led by those who are:

- seeking the Spirit's guidance together,
- able to articulate God's purposes clearly for the Church from His Word,
- drawing out regular input from the rest of the body,
- willing to face the challenge honestly, acknowledging their own preferences and even areas of "baggage",
- keen to retain what is healthy from the past,
- aware of current trends that are impacting the way the church functions,
- able to come up with creative, practical and effective strategies for the church to function according to God's intentions.

Some extra questions

To go along with the fourth question under *Life*, 'Are they learning to shape the *form* of what they do to serve whatever *function* they are convinced will lead to the *fulfilment* of God's objectives?', we can also ask:

- Are they seeing that God is not interested in empty, static, religious tradition but in something living, authentic and richly diverse?
- Are they learning to see threads in God's Narrative and to draw current applications of how He leads His people to develop forms for their function that are appropriate to the time and place?
- Are they open to the Spirit's guidance and input from others as they regularly evaluate and adjust their activities to serve the church and facilitate its witness?

The fifth question under "L" for *Life*

- Are they experiencing a deepening relationship with Jesus, learning to depend more completely on Him in different areas of their lives, and gradually seeing their values and behavior change as a result?
- Are they gaining clarity about the true purpose for which they exist, and are they increasingly able to identify those things that hinder their life in Christ?
- Are they increasingly able to make good decisions based on their understanding of God's local and global purposes, and to use their time, money and other resources accordingly?

- Are they learning to shape the *form* of what they do to serve whatever *function* they are convinced will lead to the *fulfilment* of God's objectives?

- <u>Are they growing in their commitment to reproducing the life they have in Christ, are they equipped with the resources and skills to do so, and are they prioritizing opportunities where there is real need and hunger?</u>

Producing fruit

As we noted in Tutorial 7.15, the ability to reproduce is considered one of the primary distinctives of anything that is living. Plants, for example, reach a stage where they self-propagate by dividing or producing rhizomes (shoots and runners) or by broadcasting seeds. The ability to do this demonstrates vitality and maturity. A similar principle applies to all other forms of life, including human life. And it is no stretch to make a direct link between spiritual maturity with how committed, equipped and intentional an individual believer or church is about seeing the life they have in Christ reproduced in others.

We've reflected elsewhere on the fact that authentic life in Christ produces the fruit of the Spirit such as Paul lists in Galatians 5:22. This kind of fruit is no doubt what Jesus had in mind when He said that His true disciples "produce much fruit" (John 15:8). But it seems likely He was also including another kind of yield - the "plentiful harvest of new lives" that He said elsewhere is produced when a "kernel of wheat is planted in the soil and dies" (John 12:24). In certain situations that He knows are conducive to a harvest, Jesus asks His disciples to follow Him in physical death, but in that same Galatians 5 passage, the other seemingly less dramatic kinds of fruit; "love, joy, peace, patience, kindness, goodness," etc., are also related to dying with Him on the Cross.

These regular, daily moments - "small deaths" - are not an end in themselves. Jesus didn't go to the Cross in some kind of spiritual ecstasy in the pursuit of sainthood. The very intentional commitment that took Him there was to His Father and the great Purpose for which He'd been sent into the world - opening up the way to Life for "those who are perishing". Likewise, as His followers go through the pain of "putting to death" their natural inclinations, and instead show love to people who might not be immediately loveable, when they are patient with those who try their patience, as they discipline themselves to take on challenges they wouldn't normally dream of, it should certainly be with the goal of pleasing Him, but along with that, to share His life with others. This kind of commitment - to *doing* what they need to do, *learning* what they need to know, *going* where they need to go and, most importantly, *becoming* who they need to be, in order to see His life reproduced in others - is the very essence of growth and maturity for believers.

When people with that kind of growing commitment interact with others, it is infectious. And if a number of people sharing that commitment bring together their spiritual gifts, their skills, their creativity and other resources as a church, they represent enormous potential for bringing in a "plentiful harvest of new lives". If we picture sharing God's Word in a new context, or want to form an accurate opinion of something already in process, this is obviously a key area of growth and maturity to factor in.

A careful and disciplined approach

Unfortunately, it's not uncommon for churches to be encouraging serious commitment and action from members in sharing the Gospel, but not providing any clear pathway for them to be equipped. Members are often involved in different activities and ministries, but without any real accountability to the Body as a whole. There might be prayer requests shared at a mid-week meeting or a mention in the church bulletin, but little sense of this outreach or program coming under the oversight of the leaders or being evaluated according to defined and shared Biblical values. And even for those activities that are church-sanctioned, it's all too often just a matter of looking for anyone who's willing to take it on and run things pretty much as they see fit.

If this sincere but rather haphazard approach towards local ministries is all too common, how much more so for anything that comes under the title of "missions"? Even where church leaders and their congregations are sacrificially supporting efforts to reproduce their life in Christ "out there on the mission field", it's sadly all too rare for them to feel they can or should have clearly defined benchmarks by which effectiveness is measured. Not very many have defined any theological or practical criteria for determining levels of need locally, regionally, nationally or internationally and then, in light of that, determining priorities for the use of resources entrusted to them. The "calling" of members to cross-cultural ministries is usually viewed as more a personal thing than a direct outworking of the call that Christ makes to His Church, local and global, to be vitally involved in His harvest.

The long-standing model in the West - although one which thankfully has been challenged in recent decades - is to "sub-contract" out to mission agencies all aspects of discipleship, training, sending, member care and guidance of members into overseas roles. Overworked pastors and elders are often glad to delegate the missions portfolio to others who see their role more as cheer-leaders than coaches or advisors. The further that church-supported ministries are geographically from the home area, the less likelihood there is of accountability and informed guidance being given.

None of these common weaknesses in the process of believers and churches seeing their life in Christ reproduced is inevitable or beyond repair. They can be avoided in a new context, or remedied in an existing one through the ample opportunities provided by the teaching of God's Narrative; also by a conviction from those guiding the church that clarity, thoroughness and accountability go hand in hand with enthusiasm, creativity and self-motivation. Health for an individual or group of believers is measured by their passion for Jesus and willingness to see themselves as living sacrifices for the sake of the lost. But it is also demonstrated through a careful and disciplined approach to sharing the wonderful treasure of Christ's life in ways and contexts that are most likely to bring in a harvest of new lives.

Some extra questions

To go along with the fifth question under *Life*, 'Are they growing in their commitment to reproducing the life they have in Christ, are they equipped with the resources and skills to do so, and are they prioritizing opportunities where there is real need and hunger?', we can also ask:

- Are they realizing that their willingness to associate with Jesus' death is directly linked to them having a part in His life being reproduced in others?
- Are they seeing that, whatever other helpful relationships are involved, the primary accountability structure for equipping, caring for and guiding members in ministries should come from their local church?
- Are they evaluating and aligning their efforts to share Christ's life (local or international) with the priorities, values and ministry strategies that the leadership team has clarified for the church as a whole?

FORM, FUNCTION, FULFILMENT

❓ DISCUSSION POINTS

1. Describe some of the ways that you feel the *forms* in your home church (e.g. the style of worship and other aspects of the services, smaller gatherings, the building and different ways it is used, even the degree of formality vs. casualness in interaction, dress, etc.) serve the important *functions* (e.g. equipping of members with God's Word, communal worship, discipleship, outreach of the church). Can you think of any ways the *form* could be adjusted to better serve those *functions*?

2. How directly do you believe we are meant to try to replicate the *forms* used by the early church and how much latitude is there to contextualise? How should we view any direct instructions that the apostles gave about the form of service, dress, etc.?

3. Share anything you care to about what "dying to self" looks like (areas of progress, challenges etc.) as you try to be part of seeing Jesus' life reproduced in others.

4. Carefully avoiding criticism or judgment, describe any defined frameworks or set of guidelines you know of that your church uses for determining priorities, equipping, caring for and evaluating effectiveness of church supported ministries, particularly in overseas missions.

→ ACTIVITIES

1. Picture yourself on a team that has been able to share God's Narrative with some people who are part of a large influx of refugees to your country from a strongly Islamic cultural background. Around fifteen have been saved after hearing God's Narrative from Genesis to Christ and you've taught them through Acts as well.

- Pinpoint 3-5 specific parts of the Narrative that would so far have provided Truth foundations for an understanding about form and function.
- Would you and your team (a) encourage them to integrate into an existing Bible teaching church in your area whose membership is otherwise ethnically homogenous and traditional (for your culture) OR, (b) encourage them to form their own fellowship with a distinct flavour of their original culture?
- If (a) would you encourage them adopt some/most/all the lifestyle and family practices of Christianity in the church they are joining?
- If (b) would you encourage or discourage them from bringing any of the forms related to their original culture/religion into their fellowship and Christian lives?
- If (a) or (b) would you encourage them to remain part of their refugee community if that included activities related to the mosque?

7.19 Introduction to 'Discipleship'

✓ OBJECTIVES OF THIS TUTORIAL

This tutorial introduces the fourth major area of the W.I.L.D. outline - *Discipleship* - and gives an overview from God's Word of the pattern of discipleship that is one of the major themes in God's Narrative.

Last Time

We thought about how God delights in diversity of *form* and seamlessly blends it with *function* to achieve the *fulfilment* He intends. Nowhere is this clearer than as we see Him building His Church. We considered too how growth towards maturity for believers includes discarding assumptions about how things "must" look in *form*. There are principles from God's Narrative about His perspective that come into focus in Acts and the Epistles which individuals and churches can learn to apply appropriately in their own time and place as they seek to *function* in light of God's purposes.

We also thought about how the ability to reproduce is a measure of health and maturity in all forms of life. Growth for disciples of Jesus involves an increasing willingness to give up their lives and to "die to self" in order to see His life reproduced in others. For churches, the commitment to His harvest should include a sense of responsibility for prioritizing resources, also for equipping, caring for and guiding those who go out.

So far in Module 7 we've considered "W" for *Word*, "I" for *Identity* and "L" for *Life* as lenses through which we can project or observe spiritual health and maturity. Now, in the next few tutorials, we are going to consider the last of the four W.I.L.D. areas; "D" for *Discipleship*.

What is *discipleship*?

The English word *disciple* comes to us from the Latin *discipulus*, meaning "a learner" or "pupil". The equivalent term in the Greek of New Testament times is *mathētēs* from *manthanō* (to learn). So, obviously, the idea of learning is very closely associated with *disciple*, but as we'll see, this is not the only element of meaning encompassed by the term, either in its common usage when the New Testament was being written, or in the way Jesus and his apostles themselves used it. The term *discipleship* does not appear in English translations of Scripture or indeed in most dictionaries, but it has come into common usage among Christians to describe both: (a) the relationship that exists between Jesus and His followers, and (b) the way that believers help each other in following Him. We trust that much more light will be shed on the terms *disciple* and *discipleship* as we continue.

Back in Tutorial 7.4, as we were introducing the W.I.L.D. outline, we made the point that we are not claiming any kind of inspiration for the four categories that we've used. We did explain that they've proved to be helpful and readily applicable in a wide variety of contexts, but their true validity is not based on field-testing or utility, but on whether they are categories that are grounded in the character of God; whether they are consistent with how He deals with humans; with who Jesus Christ is, and with what He is accomplishing in and through His Church. This area we're now going to trace out, *Discipleship*, is no exception. If you have made use of the AccessTruth Biblical Foundations tutorials you'll remember that a number of times through God's Narrative, we highlighted how from Creation onwards it has clearly been God's intention to have a relationship with human beings in which they look to Him for purpose, guidance and moral direction. This was to take place within the very real daily experience and responsibility of them functioning as overseers of His earthly creation.

Historical discipleship

After the Fall, it was against the backdrop of the plan of Redemption that He equipped, taught, guided and entrusted humans with responsibility, but His commitment didn't waver. The Narrative of the First Covenant is full of examples of Him "discipling" notable characters like Abraham, Joseph, Moses and David, and also many, many others we can think of. The equivalent Hebrew term *limmud,* is used only rarely, but the underlying ethos of discipleship is everywhere in the Old Testament. It's worth remembering that these teacher/learner relationships between God and individuals also extended to connections between humans in which individuals were discipled to take over a particular role: e.g. Moses and Joshua, Elijah and Elisha. It can also be said that God pursued a discipleship-like relationship with the nation of Israel, the very thing they corporately rejected when they insisted on a human monarchy to rule them. God then looked for that kind of relationship with the different kings, but it was only rare individuals - notably David - who responded in kind.

Time and space here don't allow us to do more than note in passing the historical and cultural dynamics that informed perceptions of the term *mathētēs* in New Testament times. Instances in Greek literature from the centuries before Christ included the idea of people becoming disciples of another culture, such as the Spartan way of life. It was a commitment that resulted in changes to their values and behavior. There are also many examples of people following significant masters as their disciples - philosophers such as Socrates or theoreticians like Pythagoras. Their *mathētai* (the plural form) often formed a close-knit community, learning from, adopting the perspectives, and often mimicking the mannerisms of their masters. The literature also contains mentions of individuals who were said to be a *mathētēs* of the gods: in other words, they closely aligned their beliefs and worldview to that of the gods of Greek mythology.

Judaism too, by the time of Christ, also had a number of different kinds of disciples, often called *talmidim* in Aramaic. These ranged from those who studied the Torah within a religious system like Pharisaism, followed a specific master such as Gamaliel, became adherents of one of the many prophet-type or messianic figures who rose up as popular leaders, or joined a separatist "remnant of Israel" movement such as the Qumran community, famous for copying the Scriptures down in what we know as the Dead Sea Scrolls.

Jesus' view of discipleship

When John arrived on the scene, teaching his prophetic message of repentance, baptism and a life of obedience, he not only drew curious crowds to hear his preaching, but also some individuals who followed him as disciples. Given that his ministry was to prepare for the coming Messiah, it's no surprise that some of those who'd go on to become Jesus' first disciples started out by following John. The uniqueness of Jesus' ministry and His call to discipleship were not immediately apparent to most as He began to gradually gain a following as a *rabbi* or teacher. Their perspective was shaped by their existing cultural categories for *master* and *disciple*, and also by their own worldview assumptions and commitments, and the degree to which their hearts were prepared. Many who followed did so for the wrong reasons, and even the eleven disciples who'd go on to become His apostles began with many incorrect expectations, which Jesus would increasingly challenge through His teaching and example, and even confront directly with them.

As word spread about Jesus' teaching and particularly the miracles He was performing, large numbers of people began following Him from place to place. Some were responding to His message, but many were drawn by their curiosity, aspirations and hope that He would free them from the bondage of Roman occupation. Jesus' call to follow Him was wide and inclusive; it crossed all boundaries of gender, class and ethnicity. It was "full of grace and truth", and was "contextual", in that it moved from commonalities to distinctives, from the known to the unknown. He engaged with Jewish, Old Testament kingdom aspirations but His teaching on the Kingdom of God challenged every assumption they held. He refused to let people's personal or political agendas tame down His unique call to discipleship. Following Him would not be like following another rabbi, prophetic figure, political leader or movement. He was calling them to place their faith in Him as the Messiah, the only Way to God, and to a life journey of full-on commitment to Him, no matter what the cost. As He clarified what being His disciple was all about, and as His message confronted existing worldview assumptions, it disappointed and even offended those who'd been following Him for the wrong reasons - an effect that was clearly intentional on His part (John 6:60-65).

Of course many times when the Gospel Narratives speak of "His disciples" they are referring to the twelve men who, in answer to His personal call, had left their careers and even their families for extended periods as they traveled with Him during His years of ministry. With the exception of Judas Iscariot, they had become convinced that the thirty-year-old man from Nazareth they were walking the roads of Palestine with was the Messiah, the "Holy One of God" who had "the words that give eternal life" (John 6:68–69).

The picture we're presented of these disciples that Jesus chose to be His apostles (Luke 6:13) is not of super saints or even of people who'd fully understood and submitted to all the implications of following Him from the start. They had responded to His invitation and then continued to follow Him, but it was His initiative and authority that formed the foundation for this relationship. They had no way of knowing from the outset where following Him would lead: it was His vision, His willingness to see the potential in them, His love that - in the words of 1 Corinthians 13:7 - never gave up, never lost faith, was always hopeful and endured through every circumstance. He graciously drew them along, challenging other loyalties and commitments that detracted from what *had to* become and indeed *did* become the primary relationship of their lives - being His disciples.

Careful, intentional, practical

The way Jesus went about preparing these apostles for the enormous task He would soon entrust to them was careful, intentional and practical. After speaking to the crowds He frequently spent time with the twelve explaining the Truth more fully. There are many instances of Him speaking to them as a group, but at other times He related to them individually, meeting them where they were at personally, building on strengths, speaking to their needs, confronting areas of blindness. The roads, fields, villages, encounters with people and events that took place during their time together formed the classroom in which He modelled and taught Truth. Sitting beside a vineyard became an opportunity to graphically illustrate that spiritual life and fruit is only possible through attachment to Him, the true "vine". The disciples arguing about their place in the Kingdom provided an opening to challenge their assumptions about greatness and being servants. A vicious storm on the lake became the context for a lesson in truly trusting Him as the all-powerful Creator. A conversation with a rich young man gave Him a chance to address the issue of materialism as an obstacle to true discipleship.

No doubt if we'd watched the disciples running away through the olive trees while Jesus was being arrested or, later, heard Peter, their normally bold spokesman, denying all knowledge of his Master by the fire at the High Priest's house, we would wonder if all Jesus' work with them had been in vain. But only hours before, knowing full well that they were about to temporarily abandon Him, Jesus had spoken lovingly and confidently about them to His Father. He was sending them (*apostello*) into the world, He said, in the same way *He* had been sent (John 17:18). Despite their very obvious human failings, He was confident that He had equipped them and that with God's help they would thrive.

Some seven weeks later, after Jesus' return to the Father, the Holy Spirit came to live in the apostles and continue what the Lord had begun. The Spirit's role was to help them understand and live out the implications of the Truth that Jesus had taught, and to give them the ability to go out and share the Good News that would call people into the same discipleship relationship they enjoyed with the Master.

Discipleship in the early Church

In the Church that the apostles had such a significant role in founding, the term *disciple* would become synonymous with *believer*. People in Jerusalem, the outlying areas of Israel, Samaria, Antioch, Galatia and Corinth - all those who put their faith in Jesus Christ as Saviour - would also become His disciples. Increasingly, His new disciples were people who'd never seen Him with their own eyes or heard Him speak with their own ears. In fact, before long, many who now related to Him as His disciples did not even speak Greek or Aramaic. They were from other people groups with very different cultures and locations increasingly distant from Palestine. But through a chain of disciples, each sharing the Truth about the One who came and died and rose again, and then investing their lives in those who believed, more and more came to be His followers. This was the pattern He had established: genuine relationships that see the potential in others, that intentionally encourage them to grow in their discipleship relationship with Him, that look for every opportunity to draw them into His purposes, and that help them to equip themselves for His work.

The apostle Paul, although not one of that first group who'd traveled around with Jesus, was no less a disciple, and he provides us with the best example of a discipler in the early church. His commitment to the pattern of discipleship is summed up in his exhortation to the Corinthian believers to imitate him in the same way that he imitated Christ (1 Corinthians 11:1). Paul and those who worked with him most certainly preached the Truth, but it was not all just about the proclamation of the Gospel or teaching groups of believers. He would remind the Thessalonians that, "We loved you so much that we shared with you not only God's Good News but our own lives, too" (1 Thessalonians 2:8). For Paul it was matter of personally investing in individuals as much as it was a public ministry. In the same passage to the believers in Thessalonica he said, "And you know that we treated each of you as a father treats his own children" (1 Thessalonians 2:11).

Paul and Timothy

While ministering in what was effectively his home church in Antioch in Syria or during his extensive travels, Paul almost never worked on his own. In the New Testament Narrative he's most often seen functioning as part of a church planting and strengthening team that included some younger men he was investing time and energy into. Of course the outstanding example of Paul's commitment to discipleship was his friendship with a young believer, Timothy, from the town of Lystra. The apostle met him while traveling with Silas and Luke in modern day Turkey on what we know as his second missionary journey. He invited Timothy to travel with them as they moved on to encourage the newly planted churches in the area, and then kept going as far as Philippi in Greece, where Paul left Timothy with Silas to strengthen the brand new group of believers.

Over the next couple of decades their lives and ministries would intersect many times as they traveled together, or as Paul asked his junior co-worker to take on different responsibilities among the churches, most notably in Ephesus. This, of course, is where Timothy was helping to lead the church when Paul wrote the first of his letters we have recorded in the New Testament, addressed to his "true son in the faith". The epistle includes many encouragements, exhortations and some very specific instructions that show how well Paul knew Timothy; also the sense of responsibility he took - and the freedom Timothy gave him - to speak into his life as his follower in the path of discipleship and as a discipler of others.

The second of these letters, again written from prison as Paul waits for his execution, is perhaps even more personal. He reminds Timothy of the spiritual gift he received from the Holy Spirit and encourages him to "fan the flames" of his initial experience (2 Timothy 1:6). He exhorts him to hold on to the way of teaching that Paul had shared and to carefully guard the Truth that had been entrusted to him (2 Timothy 1:13,14). And the pattern is to be repeated: the Truth that Paul has shared with him, Timothy is now to share with "other trustworthy people" (2 Timothy 2:2). And repeated again, because then they can, in turn, pass it on to others.

It's obvious that a pattern of discipleship is one of the major themes in God's Narrative: we've traced its presence right from Creation, after the Fall, through the Old Covenant times, during Jesus' life and ministry, the coming of the Spirit and then as the early Church reached out. As we picture future involvement in sharing Truth somewhere, as we evaluate proposed strategies, or if we're in a situation of evaluating the current impact of God's Word, the question of how effectively discipleship is taking place should always be a critical issue for us. The following tutorials will introduce the five questions under "D" for *Discipleship* and hopefully give us some further insights as we consider how this plays out in real contexts.

INTRODUCTION TO 'DISCIPLESHIP'

❓ DISCUSSION POINTS

1. Looking at the flow of God's Narrative, note some of the outstanding discipleship-like relationships that existed between God and individuals. What common threads with these can you trace to Jesus' discipleship when He was on earth? What are some of the factors that constitute the differences between those Old Testament relationships and us following Jesus as His disciples today?

2. Describe anything you care to about your experience and current perspective of your discipleship relationship with Jesus.

3. Can you identify any human relationships in which you have been discipled? What did those look like? Was there any intentionality about them? Were they defined in some way? Did they have any specific objectives, e.g. for a particular role?

7.20 Disciples of the Master

 OBJECTIVES OF THIS TUTORIAL

This tutorial introduces the first question in the area of *Discipleship*: 'Are they seeing all other ties, loyalties and commitments being increasingly defined by their primary relationship: disciples of their Master, Jesus Christ?'

Last time

We briefly traced the theme of *discipleship* through God's Narrative. We noted the kind of equipping and guidance He intended to give in light of the real responsibilities He entrusted to the human beings He'd created. Then we looked at how, after the Fall, this commitment played out in the relationships He pursued with individuals and the nation of Israel.

We also touched on the Greek and Jewish cultural dynamics that would have played into the New Testament term *mathētēs*, the equivalent of our English term, *disciple*. Then we thought about Jesus and His general call to the masses to follow Him as well as His specific call to the twelve men who, with one exception, would become His apostles. Also we saw the way He prepared them for the task He would entrust to them.

Finally, we considered the role of discipleship in the early Church, in particular the focus that the apostle Paul put on working with others and developing younger men in the faith like Timothy.

A framework of objectives

Once again, let's remind ourselves that in these Tutorials we are introducing a framework that's intended to help us picture something we would want to be part of; the kind of impact that, by faith, we can imagine God's Word having in the next area of ministry He leads us to. Hopefully it can help with motivation as we equip ourselves, or perhaps face leaving family and friends and moving to a new context, even to another country. Maybe it gives us ways of describing to our friends and leaders at church just what it is that we are committing to. Perhaps we will be, or already are, in a situation where we can regularly share God's Word with an individual or take a leading role in a Bible study.

Having a framework and objectives in mind should help us evaluate the impact of Truth on the individual or group so far, and then decide how to move ahead with them.

Also, as we read articles, browse ministry related websites, or have conversations about different approaches to God's work, hopefully these areas we've discussed will provide something of a filter; so we can say, "Yes, I believe this fits with what God is all about and I can incorporate it into my approach." Or, "No. If I did that, I really don't believe it would help to communicate God's Word clearly, or encourage the right sense of Identity. I can't see how that would result in vibrant, fruitful spiritual life, or really help people to follow Jesus as His disciples so they can, in turn, help others."

Obviously we don't want to take a position of 'having it all together' - we always need to keep a learner's attitude - even when we have experience to go from. But holding to convictions that are built on God's Word and the lessons His servants have learned is not wrong, and with these areas in mind it may be possible to contribute positively to conversations, even to humbly and graciously challenge assertions others are making that we might have concerns about.

The first question under "D" for *Discipleship*

- <u>Are they seeing all other ties, loyalties and commitments being increasingly defined by their primary relationship: disciples of their Master, Jesus Christ?</u>
- Are they being helped to apply the general truth from God's Word to their own specific real-life situations?
- Are they able to access regular, godly input and genuine friendships that intentionally help them along as they follow Jesus in the walk of faith?
- Are they being encouraged to function in the areas in which God has gifted and given them abilities so they can develop in their service to Him and His Body?
- Do they have access to defined pathways that offer Bible-based resources, practical instruction and relational discipleship to adequately equip them to serve the church locally and globally?

A picture of discipleship

When we talk about discipleship and particularly this first question, we're brushing up against the "Lordship salvation" controversy because its contentions are all about loyalties and commitments. The question is asked - and often answered in diametrically opposing ways, "How much commitment to Jesus Christ as Lord is required for salvation?" Our intention here is not to get embroiled in the whole debate, but we should probably identify some understandings of God's Word that frame the picture of discipleship presented here:

- God's Word clearly teaches repentance as an essential part of the new birth.
- We must take great care to guard against teaching a false gospel by mixing elements of human effort with God's grace in our description of faith's role in salvation.
- Personal acknowledgement of Jesus Christ alone, not only as Saviour but also *rightful* Lord, is a prerequisite to salvation.
- As fallen people we never completely make Jesus "Lord of all" at any point, least of all before salvation; this is legitimately part of the ongoing process of discipleship into which He calls us.
- All believers are disciples of Jesus; i.e. it is not just the realm of those who are specially committed or tagged for certain roles in the church.

Our need to relate

Human beings are relational. That's a rather obvious statement isn't it? Being poorly adjusted as a person, by definition involves some kind of difficulty in relating to others. The more extreme forms of relational problems with identifiable symptoms are given ominous sounding labels by clinical psychology: Antisocial Personality Disorder, Relationship Obsessive–Compulsive Disorder, Avoidant Personality Disorder. They all describe conditions in which people find it difficult or even impossible to relate in a "normal" way to other people. Part of being made in the image of God is the ability and urge - stronger in some than others - to *relate*. Not only to be acquainted with lots of people, to have hundreds of social media friends and followers, but to have some bonds that go deep, to share real understanding and empathy, to "know and be known".

We start out life completely reliant on others for survival. Our associations begin with simple one-way dependencies, usually in the immediate family, but as time goes by they shift and multiply...and become increasingly complex, with different levels of interdependence. Most of us only have to cast our minds back to our school years to be reminded of just how dramatic and fraught relationships can be, or at least seem, at that stage of life. This is magnified exponentially when the opposite sex shifts in our eyes from being a despised sub-race to something worth pursuing and wooing. And it never really seems to stop, this process of adding to and managing an intricate web of different types of relationships. We're always relating in some way: to the guy at the service station where we regularly fill up, our accountant, the other parents at our kids' school, old friends we keep in contact with through social media, work colleagues, the leaders at church, grown up siblings, aging parents, spouses.

Taken from one viewpoint, that's exactly what human life is - a personal network of dependencies, commitments, obligations, unresolved conflicts, loyalties, affections etc. And societies are an extension or amalgamation of all these relationships into some kind of definable unit. Societies and communities represent the idea of the individual in a relationship with an entire group; of people connected by a shared identity, ideals (e.g. equality, freedom, opportunity), religious beliefs, or even racial superiority (usually with disastrous results). In some situations this relationship to a society plays out as patriotism that, conditioned by training and loyalty to a smaller unit of comrades-in-arms, is strong enough to motivate individuals to give up their lives for the sake of their country. A particularly destructive form of extreme loyalty to a sub-group within society has become known as *tribalism* (e.g. Political corruption that ensures the dominance of a particular ethnic group), or *neo-tribalism*, (e.g. Hooligan supporters of certain European football teams.) Religious cults prey on the human inclination towards dependent relationships and loyalties, binding adherents together under authoritarian rule, esoteric understanding and a fabricated sense of being under siege from the rest of the world.

But even at a less extreme level, there's a nearly infinite variety of voices constantly clamouring for our loyalties: "Invest exclusively with our bank." "Give to our worthy cause." "Sign up to our rewards program." "Eat our hamburgers." "Use our website." More traditional societies with less exposure to corporate advertising are, if anything, even more reliant on a network of dependencies and loyalties. Fishermen need the goodwill of market stallholders to sell their catch while it's fresh. The rural family that keeps three cows depends on the rickshaw driver who comes around to collect the morning's milk. Farmers rely on the local store owner to give rice and kerosene on credit in lean times, to be paid back after the harvest. Today's successful hunter, knowing that next time his family will benefit from someone else's good fortune, distributes wild pig meat in the village. When a child is sick you might need the help of the workers at the clinic and then, just to be sure, take a chicken over to the old lady who knows the chants for this kind of fever.

A discipleship relationship with Jesus

We're reminding ourselves just how important and all-pervasive relationships are at every level of human life, because this is obviously very relevant when we consider what a growing discipleship relationship with Jesus looks like. People's initial encounter with His call to discipleship never occurs in a relational vacuum. Whether they finally hear Him after a gradual increase in volume over a period of time or as a loud, dramatic summons, the call always emerges above a chorus of other voices demanding their attention and devotion. This has always been the case. Abraham was a son, a brother, a husband, the head of a household, and a member of a community, when God began to draw him into His purposes. David's immensely rewarding, if occasionally painful, walk with God began in the context of his family, and continued through his relationship with Saul, Jonathan, his band of fighters, the prophet Samuel, the nation of Israel, and his wives and children. We're not told what Zebedee thought when his sons James and John left him alone to mend nets in response to Jesus' invitation to follow Him, but family obligations must have featured strongly for these fishermen as they followed the Master and became His apostles.

In the weeks and months that followed that first call, the disciples would hear Jesus directly address the issue of relationships that compete with being His disciple. Probably the most dramatic instance is in Luke 14:26 when He said "If you want to be my disciple, you must hate everyone else by comparison - your father and mother, wife and children, brothers and sisters." Of course we need to read this in its context and remember that He was addressing a large group, many of whom were following Him for the wrong reasons. And we know from the rest of God's Word that He wasn't talking about how people can be made right with God. We also know from the Narrative and Jesus' own teaching that He wasn't denigrating the family; He wasn't saying that people shouldn't honor their parents or love their spouses and children. But He *was* making the point that being His disciple involves a willingness to place all other connections, allegiances and duties in a lower priority to a relationship with Him.

But this is not a simple matter of mathematics; of calculating that Jesus is getting a bit more of our time, money or energy than anyone else. We've already noted just how much "normal" human life is defined by an incredibly complex, multi-layered tangle of connections, affiliations, friendships and bonds. Human hearts and minds are not equipped to evaluate all of that objectively; they're unable to wash away the subtle motivations, the insecurities, the pride, the lusts, the unhealthy dependencies, jealousies, and miscommunication that have been the grit in the cogs of all human relationships since the Fall. As zealous as a new disciple might be about making Jesus "Lord of all their lives", they don't yet know Him or themselves well enough to do that. But their zeal isn't misplaced, because He honours this and through His Spirit, His Word, and other disciples He gladly takes on the task of realigning all other relationships according to this one they've now entered into with Him. His desire is not to add to the weight of futile obligations and guilt that many people come to Him with, but rather to lighten it by taking it from them. Discipleship costs, but the relationship with Him itself is not a heavy burden. Instead it's like a yoke or harness that allows His disciples to walk alongside Him, learning from Him, and experiencing peace and rest as they get to know a Master who is truly "humble and gentle at heart" (Matt. 11:28-30).

The challenges of discipleship

Salvation often brings with it added relational pressures as a new believer faces changes in how family members, friends and acquaintances view them. We'll talk more in subsequent tutorials about the role of other believers in *discipleship*, but we should note here just how invaluable it is for someone in that situation to get help from another disciple who's a little further down the road. We know that once God has brought someone into His family on the basis of their faith in Jesus' sacrifice, He will never give them up; but tragically there are numerous examples of His children who never move far at all along the road of discipleship. There's a very real chance of them giving up right at the beginning when they take their first faltering steps and immediately face the challenge of dealing with a whole network of existing relationships and competing loyalties. Without anyone to help them see how their new relationship with Jesus can provide all the comfort and insights they so desperately need right now, they can wrongly see it as another whole set of obligations and commitments they feel inadequate for. Facing this on their own, there's every chance they'll simply give up, with the very real possibility of never really knowing the exciting privilege and responsibilities of being Jesus' disciples.

At the same time, a danger for new believers is that, instead of coming to see their connection with Jesus as the relationship that defines all others, they give that role to an individual, group or church that has been instrumental in them coming to faith. No doubt we've all seen amusing pictures of a hen, for example, being followed around by young that are clearly from a bigger species of bird, like geese or ducks. When they hatched from the egg, an instinctive bond was immediately created with the first living thing they saw. Similarly, a new believer, feeling emotionally vulnerable and also, understandably, grateful to those who've nurtured their faith, can mistakenly give their primary allegiance to others who in reality are also needy disciples of Jesus just like themselves.

Those who take on the role of teaching Truth and bringing others to Christ, must be very conscious of this danger and proactively work against it. We've all seen the dangers of the cult of personality and celebrity within evangelical circles and the pitfalls of believers putting their faith in individuals. The same is true of denominations, churches, para-church organisations, mission agencies, Christian educational facilities and programs when, often unintentionally, they attract loyalty and dependency that should rightfully be given only to the Lord Jesus Christ.

As we perhaps envisage our own involvement in a situation where we have opportunity to share God's Word with individuals or a group of people and see them come to faith, the picture we should have in mind is of us introducing them to Jesus and then, once they've become His disciples, cheering them on as they walk alongside and grow in Him. In our own relationship as disciples of the Master, we need to keep asking for

His help to avoid the subtle temptation of wanting people to follow *us*, of making a personal commitments to *us*, of finding their needs met in *us*. Likewise, those involved in leading churches and ministry teams, must avoid the trap of conflating or confusing true discipleship with people becoming *their* members, *their* converts. For those who take on roles of guiding others, the real measure of their success is how much they are able to help others follow Jesus. The way they do this is through their words, but far more influentially, as they show their own loyalty to Him and His Cause by what they prioritise and value in their lives.

Some extra questions

To go along with the first question in the area of *Discipleship*, 'Are they seeing all other ties, loyalties and commitments being increasingly defined by their primary relationship: disciples of their Master, Jesus Christ?', we can also ask:

- Are they realizing that the relationship with Jesus is unique from all others in terms of its scope and rightful claims, and because it gives them access to His guidance in handling all other relationships correctly?
- Are new believers being given help by other disciples as they face the challenges of reconfiguring their existing personal commitments and obligations in light of the relationship they've entered into with Jesus?
- Are the individuals or teams in discipleship roles truly encouraging other believers in their commitments to Jesus as Master, or are they - perhaps unknowingly - fostering unhealthy individual and corporate allegiances?

? DISCUSSION POINTS

1. What are some of the things you'd say to a new believer who asked for your advice about how they should relate to an unbelieving partner, now that they are following Jesus? Would you have any helpful examples to share from your own experience of relating to others as a disciple?

2. Describe some of the concrete things that you feel a church should (a) avoid (b) do, to encourage members to give their primary allegiance as disciples to Jesus, rather than to individuals or to the church.

3. Do you feel there is an appropriate, healthy level of loyalty that someone can give to a group, Christian organization, church etc.? Also comment on any factors, circumstances or cultural trends that play into this for many today, especially the younger generation.

→ ACTIVITIES

1. Do some research and reading on the "Lordship salvation" debate, then in less than a page:

(a) summarize the salient points of contention,

(b) briefly explain your own perspective/standpoint,

(c) share any comments or questions you might have about any of the five bulleted points made early in this tutorial that undergird the picture of discipleship presented in these resources.

7.21 Applying Truth in the walk of faith

 OBJECTIVES OF THIS TUTORIAL

This tutorial introduces the second and third questions in the area of *Discipleship*: 'Are they being helped to apply the general Truth from God's Word to their own specific real-life situations?' and 'Are they able to access regular, godly input and genuine friendships that intentionally help them along as they follow Jesus in the walk of faith?'

Last time

We started out with five points that clarify some understandings of God's Word that frame the picture of discipleship presented in these resources. We then thought about the fact that people live within a complex network of connections, relationships and dependencies. When some do hear Jesus' call to follow Him as Saviour and Master, it is not in a vacuum, but against the background of all of the other voices that are trying to forge links and allegiances. Jesus wants His disciples to put His relationship with them first, but His intention is not to add to the existing burden of relationships but rather to bear it with those who follow Him.

We also thought about how new believers need help from others as they learn to relate to everyone on the basis of their new identity as disciples of Jesus. Anyone taking on the role of discipling others needs to be careful they are encouraging allegiances and commitments to Jesus rather than to themselves or their group.

The second question under "D" for *Discipleship*

- Are they seeing all other ties, loyalties and commitments being increasingly defined by their primary relationship: disciples of their Master, Jesus Christ?

- <u>Are they being helped to apply the general truth from God's Word to their own specific real-life situations?</u>

- Are they able to access regular, godly input and genuine friendships that intentionally help them along as they follow Jesus in the walk of faith?

- Are they being encouraged to function in the areas in which God has gifted and given them abilities so they can develop in their service to Him and His Body?
- Do they have access to defined pathways that offer Bible-based resources, practical instruction and relational discipleship to adequately equip them to serve the church locally and globally?

Practical outcomes in the real world

As we've noted a number of times before, God is not interested in religion, theological study, doctrinal orthodoxy or Scriptural knowledge *as ends in themselves*. Under the Old Covenant He spoke dismissively of people whose hearts are far away even while they're honoring Him with their words, and whose "worship" is just man-made rules they've memorized (Isaiah 29:13). The apostle Paul talked about people who are always pursuing new teaching but never really coming to a genuine understanding of the Truth (2 Timothy 3:7). Elsewhere he drew a contrast between *knowledge* that does little else than make us feel important, and *love* that has the practical outcome of strengthening the church (1 Corinthians 8:1). In that same epistle he makes a similar contrast in the famous "love chapter" when he says, "If I had the gift of prophecy, and if I understood all of God's secret plans and possessed all knowledge, and if I had such faith that I could move mountains, but didn't love others, I would be nothing." (1 Corinthians 13:2).

This is not to say that understanding, knowledge, or theory is unimportant, but only that it is fruitless without practical outcomes in the real world. This takes us back to a previous discussion about *form*, *function* and *fulfilment*. From the beginning, God's dealings with people always addressed the very real circumstances of their lives, with the goal of them knowing how He wanted them to live and what He wanted them to achieve.

The example of David

Among numerous examples in God's Narrative, we get a great picture of this in the way He interacted with David throughout his life, particularly through the prophets Samuel, and later, Nathan. God had an amazing plan for the youngest son of Jesse and we know that he'd go on to have a pivotal role in the history of Israel; he'd also contribute through many of the Psalms to God's written Narrative; he was the prominent human ancestor in the Messiah's royal lineage and for countless generations David has provided a prime example of a human being relating to the Lord. As that story unfolds, we see clearly that this Hebrew person God chose to be part of His purposes and who He even called "a man after my own heart" (1 Samuel 13:14 and Acts 13:22), was a very real human being with weaknesses and needs. But he also loved God's Word deeply as he would express poignantly in worship songs like this, "How I delight in your commands! How I love them! I honor and love your commands. I meditate on your decrees." (Psalm 119:47,48)

Although the interaction between God and David was very much on a spiritual level (e.g. Psalm 51:10,11 "Renew a loyal spirit within me...don't take your Holy Spirit from me.") it wasn't only that - it played out in the very real world of bitter enmity and sweet friendship, triumph and defeat, zeal for God and horrendous sin, love and lust, mercy and murder. Often God's communication with David was through His designated mouthpieces, His prophets. The first was Samuel who was sent to anoint the young man as Saul's successor. Later, to escape from the enraged king, David went and lived with Samuel in Ramah. We can only surmise that the aged prophet might have been used during this time by God to teach more of His Truth to the future monarch of His people, perhaps in what might even be described as a discipleship relationship.

But it was Nathan, the next of Israel's prophets, who would have the task of passing on some very direct communication from God to David. It was through Nathan that the Lord told David he should prepare for the building of the Jerusalem temple. After David's adultery with Bathsheba, and the arranged killing of her husband Uriah, it was Nathan that God sent to rebuke the king. And later the prophet would warn David of his son Adonijah's plot to take the throne in place of Solomon. Without doubt, David loved the Lord and His Word, but the nature of God and the justice of His Law were not just concepts to be discussed over a glass of wine with Samuel or for meditation in the mountains while strumming a harp. He needed to learn their reality in light of day-to-day struggles and realities of his own human weakness. Once or twice he might have been given a prophetic glimpse of God's Messianic purposes, but those were being enacted right now in the dust and sweat of work, in the blood of battle, and in decisions that would have a real impact on the future of the nation entrusted to him.

The Example of Jesus and His disciples

When it comes to examples in God's Word of His people being helped to apply Truth to their own circumstances, we need look no further than Jesus and His disciples. Just one instance among many is found in Matthew 10 in a briefing session before He sends them out to tell their fellow Israelites that the Kingdom of God is at hand. In Matthew's concise account - just 36 verses of instructions - Jesus touches on abstract concepts like God's love and care for them, but also very down to earth applications to do with money and clothing. He shares a glimpse of future challenges that must have filled them with excitement, but also terror - they'd stand trial before governors and kings, nations would hate them - but then moments later He gives detailed directions about what they should do in the next few days if people in a nearby town don't listen to their message.

Of course by this stage, when He has singled them out to name them as His apostles and is sending them out on a short-term mission, they have already been with Him as part of the larger group of followers for some time. They've heard Him teach from the Scriptures in the synagogues and to crowds by the lake. They've seen Him interacting with people of all kinds: earnest seekers, half-hearted followers, antagonistic religious leaders. They've heard Him describe His relationship to the Father. They have at least some perspective of what was involved in being His disciples. So now He's building on the foundations of Truth already there and counting on the model of His own life that they have had opportunity to learn from.

All of that has been their classroom that has mixed theory with some practical realities, but now they are going to be sent out on their own to get their feet wet, or perhaps to briefly "jump in the deep end". They are moving from just being His disciples (learners) to also being His apostles (sent ones). Now they get to put His teaching and instruction into practice; in the context of real life, doing an actual task. They'll need to apply the Truth they've heard in their relationships as co-workers with each other, in the face of rejection or indifference to the Message, to trust God for their food and somewhere to sleep. For now this is just practice; it won't be long and they'll be back with Him, debriefing, telling Him everything that happened to them out there (Luke 9:10). But He knows that in just a few short months He will be authorizing them for the real Task that He's equipping them for. Then they will be responsible to pass on to others all He was now teaching them, not only to fellow Jews who share so much background of Truth, but also to make disciples among the "unreached" Gentile people groups.

Is teaching discipleship?

It is sometimes debated whether teaching - i.e. the exposition of God's Word to a group - is legitimately discipleship. In fact, it's probably unnecessary to draw too sharp a distinction between them. God's Word, as well as experience, tell us that teaching for the gathered church is indispensable. There's also a valid place for the classroom, the conference and the retreat, with some very real benefits to having a group processing instruction together. But certain factors (e.g. the size of the group, how formal or interactive the dynamics are, how well the teacher knows the audience, how well the audience knows each other, how culturally and generationally homogenous the group is, how much shared teaching from God's Word they've had, how close they are in maturity, etc.) come into play.

So, with that in mind, perhaps a helpful statement can be made along these lines: *Teaching moves towards discipleship as it becomes <u>less</u> formal, theoretical, general, and detached, with <u>more</u> personal application, discussion, interaction and access to personal relationships.*

As these AccessTruth resources themselves, by nature of their form, are more theoretical, general and without recourse to direct interaction or personal relationships, we rely on those who make use of them (whether they're being equipped or helping to equip others) to bring in a discipleship element. That serves as an example for any teaching situation that is strong on theory but short on personal application. The *form* in which teaching takes place should be regularly evaluated in this light and, where possible, adjustments made to serve the *function* and eventual *fulfilment* of discipleship. In many situations, such as these materials, additional opportunities have to be made so that somehow, someone who is further down the road of discipleship with Jesus is helping others coming behind to consider the real-life implications of the Truth and practical instruction they are getting. That process, as we've already seen in the examples of David's walk with God and the apostles' with Jesus, is only really effective when the applications of Truth are not an end in themselves but part of the disciple being drawn into and equipped for God's purposes - being discipled to make disciples.

Some extra questions

To go along with the second question in the area of *Discipleship*, 'Are they being helped to apply the general Truth from God's Word to their own specific real-life situations?', we can also ask:

- As they read, study, or hear God's Word being taught, do they see it as communication from a real Person who's always there and vitally interested in their daily lives, or is it more a religious activity they're participating in?
- Is there a conscious effort being made to evaluate and, where possible, adjust the form in which Truth is taught to the gathered church so that it encourages discipleship in the body?
- Are there opportunities made for smaller groups (including one-on-one scenarios) to process, discuss and make relevant, practical applications from the teaching that is being given to the whole church?

The third question under "D" for *Discipleship*

- Are they seeing all other ties, loyalties and commitments being increasingly defined by their primary relationship: disciples of their Master, Jesus Christ?
- Are they being helped to apply the general truth from God's Word to their own specific real-life situations?
- <u>Are they able to access regular, godly input and genuine friendships that intentionally help them along as they follow Jesus in the walk of faith?</u>
- Are they being encouraged to function in the areas in which God has gifted and

given them abilities so they can develop in their service to Him and His Body?

- Do they have access to defined pathways that offer Bible-based resources, practical instruction and relational discipleship to adequately equip them to serve the church locally and globally?

How does discipleship take place?

We said earlier that when we use the term *discipleship* we're encapsulating two related aspects:

a) The relationship that exists between Jesus and His followers.
b) The way that believers help each other in following Him.

In light of that simple definition, we can say that the more someone knows Jesus, has learned from Him, and is working closely with Him, the more able they are to help His other disciples do likewise.

The picture we should have of discipleship is of all His people aligned to follow Him, but with each on a unique path as He disciples them within the reality of their personal story, social context, gifts and abilities, and of course how they respond to Him. But how does Jesus disciple them now that He's not physically on the earth? Well, we know it's through His Word as they have access to it (look back at Tutorial 7.6 for thoughts on what that *access* involves) and through His Spirit relating to their hearts and minds. But as we've noted many times, He graciously chooses to use human beings in His purposes, and this is most certainly true of discipleship. So in our mental image, we should picture each of His disciples on their own individual path, but with Him directing those paths to make multiple intersections with others. And in these convergences of His people, these relationships that are sometimes for a season and sometimes for a lifetime, He advances His discipleship goals for each of those involved.

As Romans 8:28 says, "we know that God causes everything to work together for the good of those who love God and are called according to His purpose for them." This is true of every "chance" encounter, acquaintance and relationship. In His sovereign wisdom He is able to teach His children lessons through every interaction, even the ones that seem to have no purpose or are perhaps painful. So from His side - what we've described as (a) in our brief definition - all of those "intersections" of paths potentially contribute to what He intends for each disciple. But He also wants to involve them in a positive contribution, a purposeful cooperation, with Him in this process, the part that (b) in our definition refers to.

This aspect of discipleship - i.e., the part that Jesus' disciples themselves can play - is all about relationships. There are some rare instances of brief, life-changing conversations between relative strangers, and many believers are impacted by the testimonies of His servants down through history who they've never met in person, but as a rule the most meaningful and worthwhile interactions take place within relationships. By "relationships" we mean when there is enough time spent together to develop significant trust and openness. As we all know, those kinds of relationships, or *friendships*, don't just happen; they require both sides putting in the effort to develop and maintain them. But what is the difference between a standard, "common or garden" friendship and a genuine discipleship relationship? The wording of the W.I.L.D. question we're considering here addresses this by bringing *intention* or *intentionality* into the frame. That doesn't necessarily mean "planned", "structured" or "scheduled" - although none of those is inherently at odds with relational discipleship, as we'll discuss later.

Intentional discipleship

Jesus' relationship with His disciples was a real one and we definitely see a genuine love and affection for these men coming through the Narrative. But He also had very clearly defined goals for His three years with them, as we can tell from what He reviews with the Father near the end of that time (John 17):

- reveal God to them (v. 6),
- pass on His message to them (v. 8),
- protect and guard them (v. 12),
- tell them things that will fill them with joy (v. 13),
- give them God's Word (v. 14),
- send them into the world (v. 18),
- unite them around a shared experience of God's glory (v. 22).

And His objectives for them were not only broad and generic. From the personal exchanges recorded in the Gospels it's not difficult to infer at least some of the specific areas in their lives He was helping them both to recognise and to grow in. Peter's impulsiveness, overconfidence and tendency to speak before thinking provide obvious examples, but there were many other instances of Jesus specifically addressing failures to trust Him, ambitiousness, narrow-mindedness, selfishness, etc.

Of course that was Jesus, right? He was God after all, and the disciples were following Him because they believed He was the Messiah. He had the right to identify and address areas of need in others. But how can His disciples today, conscious of their human weaknesses and sin, be confident that they can disciple someone else? Certainly the current of Western culture is against the idea of that kind of intentionality within a relationship; and not without good reason. There has been so much abuse of authority and people using their positions to manipulate and dominate others, that many are wary of taking on the role of discipling others. This caution is a healthy one as long as it isn't crippling - certainly if someone has *not* wrestled with the question of exactly what gives them the right to disciple others, then they really aren't qualified to take that role.

But by faith, we have to be convinced that it is possible, despite all the human frailties involved, for there to be healthy discipleship relationships, genuine friendships that are also intentional. In some situations it is even profitable to have that defined; for someone younger in the faith to specifically welcome a brother or sister further along in their walk with the Lord to play that discipleship or *mentoring* role with them. In certain contexts, where someone is being equipped for a wider role in God's work, it can even be appropriate to have this take place within a structured program, with scheduled times together and predetermined topics to work through. But the dynamics in those more formalised situations create significant challenges that, although not insurmountable, require extra sensitivity and effort if it is to be truly a profitable friendship and not just part of a course or weekly schedule to tick off as "completed" in a "Leaders' guide" or on a productivity app.

Some of the essential ingredients that allow for intentionality within a discipleship relationship while guarding against it becoming unhealthy or just a form to be followed are: humility, genuine care and empathy, the desire to listen more than to speak, the ability to really hear what someone might have trouble articulating in words, and experience in following Jesus while putting faith into practice. Trust is the lifeblood of discipleship; without someone who is trustworthy and someone to trust them, discipleship doesn't take place. The trust has to be well founded and tested by the passing of some time, through the normal give and take of a relationship, in open, honest conversations, through vulnerability and through shared experiences.

But as we see through God's Narrative, and as experience teaches, effective discipleship doesn't happen in a vacuum. Intentional, relational discipleship is only really effective when there is a sense of a shared cause and purpose for the relationship. And the intention cannot only be one way. At very least, the starting point has to be a shared desire to follow Jesus more closely. Then, as time goes by and with His help, other more specific objectives can naturally emerge that give focus and incentive for both sides of the relationship. The "shared cause" then doesn't outgrow individual spiritual growth, but it begins to take on broader aspects related to God's local and global purposes. Further questions could be explored such as: what part does Jesus want this disciple of His to play? How has He gifted him or her? What ongoing equipping could they pursue? What are the values that will shape their lives and contribution to the Task? How can *they* themselves build discipleship relationships with others? But where discipleship is most effective and fulfilling, is where the relationship actually develops "on the job" into genuine equality and a partnership of mutually trusted co-workers.

Some extra questions

To go along with the third question in the area of *Discipleship*, 'Are they able to access regular, godly input and genuine friendships that intentionally help them along as they follow Jesus in the walk of faith?' we can also ask:

- Is the subject of relational discipleship being taught and discussed in a way that communicates its true value and necessity in the life of individuals and the group?
- Are there those who, although very conscious of their own needs, are actively pursuing friendships with other believers with the purpose of encouraging them to follow Him as disciples?
- Are there opportunities for discipleship relationships to develop into genuine partnerships of equality and trust in the context of service?

Amber's Story

Amber was a bit nervous but also excited; finally she was going to be involved in what she had been thinking about and preparing to do for so long - discipleship in Africa! It had been arranged for her to go twice a week and spend time teaching typing and computer skills, but also to help disciple girls at a vocational school. These girls from the poorest of poor families had been given this opportunity by a church-sponsored program to escape life in the slums, and she'd been told that they'd all made professions of faith.

Waiting at the bus stop among ladies in vivid dresses and matching head scarves, Amber reflected on the journey that had brought her here. It had all started when she was 17 and a missionary couple, working in West Africa, had come to her home church to speak to the youth group. She had been impacted by their challenge to obey Jesus' command to make disciples and from then on she'd planned to do that in Africa. Her church leadership had been encouraging but recommended that she get some training first. At her Christian college she'd majored in Intercultural Studies, but her real passion had become discipleship. She'd researched then written an extensive paper on the subject and later, as she went about partnership development in her own church and elsewhere, she'd always highlighted discipleship as the thing she wanted to be involved in. When an opportunity came along to work with a church in Kano, the second biggest city in Nigeria, she'd jumped at it. Now, after settling in for four months in this huge bustling city, the senior pastor had asked if she would help out at the vocational school.

Yesterday, after the Sunday service, the pastor had introduced her to a lady with a disfiguring facial scar that she'd shared 'hellos' with at church but never actually spoken to. He said that Precious already knew the girls at the school and they'd be going there together the two days each week. Now, as Amber watched her approach along the crowded footpath, the thought crossed her mind that the Lord might have put them together regularly so she could encourage and disciple Precious.

On the hour long bus trip to their destination near Bagwai dam, Amber was surprised to find that Precious already knew each of the girls from the vocational school by name, and was able to provide some invaluable information about their background and educational levels. But more than that, she seemed to really care for them as individuals. Later that afternoon saying goodbye, it struck Amber that for the whole bus trip back to the city she'd been responding to gentle questions about how she'd found the first day and her impressions of the girls.

And that set the pattern for their two hour conversations each Monday and Thursday. She'd never wanted to be one of those people who just talk about themselves, but somehow Amber found herself opening up in a way she never really had with anyone else. It wasn't that Precious didn't share anything about herself. Over the next months her story emerged; that she and her husband were actually from a people group in the neighboring country of Chad; and how, after their extended family had turned to Christ, their grass thatched houses had been torched at night and it was then her face had been badly burned. They also talked about the couple's dreams of being part of a church planting effort in their home area. But it was Amber's life that seemed to feature much more in the conversations; her turbulent adolescent years as her parents' marriage dissolved in acrimony, her desire to serve the Lord, the occasional bouts of loneliness she was experiencing here in Nigeria, even the kind of man she was looking for. They'd talk about the messages at church or what they'd read themselves in the Bible, and about what exactly it means for a young woman to follow Jesus as His disciple.

The other topic that Precious came back to most mornings as they rode out of town on the A9 and then on to dusty, bumpy rural roads, was the girls at the vocational school. What growth could they see in them? How could they help them in their walk with Jesus? How could they be real friends to them? Amber realized after a while that her picture of discipleship had changed. It wasn't that all the theory she'd written into her college papers - in what already seemed a lifetime ago - was wrong. And they still had the "Discipleship Hour" before Computer Class that she'd established in her first week, but it looked quite different to how she'd once imagined it. Watching Precious relate to the girls and seeing how they warmed to her, how they liked hanging out with her, how they opened up with occasional tears but with laughter ever present, how they listened so intently when she shared something from the Word or brought her own relationship with the Lord naturally into the conversation…this was now the predominant image in Amber's mind when she thought of discipleship.

They'd been traveling to the school together for more than 18 months when Precious told her one morning that she and her husband were leaving Kano to go back to their home area in Chad. He'd finished his training as a translator and now they would be part of a Bible translation project in the language they'd grown up with. Amber was excited for them, knowing this had been on their hearts for years, but she realized she'd miss her friend deeply in the days ahead. On the bus alone a few weeks later, she smiled at the memory of that first morning when she'd prayed for an opportunity to disciple the lady with the scarred face walking towards her. In fact, it dawned on her now for the first time, that she had been the one who'd been helped most in following Jesus. Yes, she hoped she'd been some small encouragement to Precious, but she had learned far, far more than she had taught. Maybe, just maybe, she thought as she looked out the window at men in shiny suits on bicycles and ladies sitting under umbrellas selling oranges, she might just be ready to disciple others now herself.

❓ DISCUSSION POINTS

1. In your own words describe a scenario in which members of a church are helped to apply teaching from God's Word in ways that relate directly to their daily situations. Is this mainly hypothetical for you or have you actually participated in something that you believe effectively moved towards discipleship in this way?

2. Imagine that you are serving in another country and have been asked to fill a role equivalent to "Dean of students" for your own gender at a Bible college. One of your stated responsibilities is to spend at least an hour each week in a discipleship session. What are some specific prayer points you think you might include in an email to your support network back home as you start into this new role?

3. Do you agree with the assertion that "Discipleship doesn't happen in a vacuum"? Please give your reasons and explain what you believe it means.

4. In Amber's story, what do you think might have been her picture of discipleship before meeting Precious and in what key ways do you suspect it had shifted after their months together?

7.22 Equipped for service

 OBJECTIVES OF THIS TUTORIAL

This tutorial introduces the fourth and fifth questions in the area of *Discipleship*: 'Are they being encouraged to function in the areas in which God has gifted and given them abilities so they can develop in their service to Him and His Body?' and 'Do they have access to defined pathways that offer Bible-based resources, practical instruction and relational discipleship to adequately equip them to serve the church locally and globally?'

Last time

We considered how God is committed, not only to communicating Truth, but also to helping His people know how to live it out in real ways that contribute to His purposes.

We looked at the example of David and how God's interaction with him was not only on a sacred, spiritual level, but also in the real challenges, victories and even failures of life. We also highlighted how these same principles worked out in Jesus' relationship with His disciples as He shared the big, overarching truths about God with them but also gave very down to earth, specific instructions in light of the task He was equipping them for.

We then focused on the way Jesus wants to use relationships between His disciples to help them in following Him. We briefly considered what it might look like to have genuine, healthy friendships that are intentional but without being manipulative or overbearing.

The fourth question under "D" for *Discipleship*

- Are they seeing all other ties, loyalties and commitments being increasingly defined by their primary relationship: disciples of their Master, Jesus Christ?
- Are they being helped to apply the general truth from God's Word to their own specific real-life situations?

- Are they able to access regular, godly input and genuine friendships that intentionally help them along as they follow Jesus in the walk of faith?

- Are they being encouraged to function in the areas in which God has gifted and given them abilities so they can develop in their service to Him and His Body?

- Do they have access to defined pathways that offer Bible-based resources, practical instruction and relational discipleship to adequately equip them to serve the church locally and globally?

Disciples of Christ working together

The picture of discipleship we've been developing here is of Jesus leading His followers on their own unique paths as He calls and encourages them to walk with Him. He is eager for them to see themselves "yoked" or bonded to Him, not to add to the burdens of life, but so He can share them. Following a Master who sacrificed everything for others does involve giving some things up, but they are things that won't last anyway, and what is gained is eternal. Even though disciples follow individual paths, they regularly intersect with others briefly or for a lifetime; sometimes being *helped*, sometimes *helping*, and most often *helping each other* to follow Jesus.

As we consider the fourth question under "Discipleship" we want to add some more detail to that picture, focusing in on how the Lord brings a number of His disciples' paths together for His purposes. At times groups of disciples work together for specific projects or specialised aspects of His Commission to make disciples to the "ends of the earth", but by far the most important convergences are when they come together as local churches. Whatever connotations "church" might have, particularly in individualistic, consumerist cultures, from God's perspective these *disciple gatherings* are not a matter of chance or just personal preference for things like worship styles. Somehow, He's able to give genuine freedom of choice to His disciples while, at the same time, sovereignly blending their gifts and abilities so as to give the best opportunity for individuals to thrive and for the group to serve His purposes.

But as we've noted many times, God pursues genuine partnerships with His people, and this is no more true than in the process of individual disciples being encouraged to use the gifts and abilities He's given them within the local Body and as it reaches out. As we picture how an existing or future ministry might develop, when we hear others talk about programs and strategies, or if we're trying to get a clear view of an existing situation, this is a critical area to include. Here are the kinds of relevant questions we might ask ourselves depending on the context:

Am I committed to helping other disciples of Jesus thrive in areas He has gifted them for, even if it means them overtaking me and being more appreciated than I am?

Is our concept of "the team" a healthy, Biblical one or does it unthinkingly exclude brothers and sisters based on extraneous factors like education, background, ethnicity, etc?

Does this model take people out of the context of the church and train them to an elite status that only a few can hope to attain at the risk of stifling other potential within the Body?

Is this situation such that someone might be concerned about losing status, control, even financial security, if they really encourage others to function fully in their area of gifts and abilities?

Do the leaders of the church have a proactive strategy for offering real opportunities for service, identifying those best suited, and ensuring that they are equipped and discipled for those roles?

Perhaps these few questions serve to highlight the reality that an atmosphere in which Jesus' disciples are consistently encouraged to function in areas for which they're gifted doesn't just happen as a matter of course. Often the obstacles are a *personal* lack of awareness and vision, or even simple indifference and laziness. After all, it takes real commitment and willingness to invest time and energy into someone else who may or may not respond as we believe they should. The possibility of frustration and personal disappointment is not something everyone is able to face, especially if they apply a "once bitten twice shy" principle. Often too, it really does seem more efficient and easier to follow another dictum, "If you want to do the job well, do it yourself."

But Jesus would not have entrusted the founding of His Church to the apostles and its building to subsequent generations of disciples if He took that approach. Within that initial group of twelve followers He dealt with immaturity, lack of faith, cowardice and even outright betrayal. And down through history since He has been willing to graciously persist with disciples, not one of whom has ever completely fulfilled their potential or used their gifts as they might have. Obviously though, He knows that the investment is worth the cost; the reward of finally seeing a disciple step up to the plate of His Cause makes up for all the disappointments; every choice to serve beats a thousand failures to respond, hands down.

Discipleship functioning in the church

At times the obstacles are not so much personal as *systemic*. In many settings history has played a significant role in shaping beliefs and assumptions about *ecclesiology* - i.e. theology applied to the nature and structure of the Church. Even within what are called *evangelical* circles (a term that has lost much of its definition in recent times) there exists a wide range of models, from the highly organised and hierarchical to the amorphous and unstructured. Without taking the time and space here to trace this out, we can see how both extremes are often not conducive to disciples of Jesus being encouraged to function in areas for which they have the gifts and abilities. In general, churches with a strong emphasis on structure also tend to preserve influential roles for those few with formal theological and academic qualifications. At the other end of the spectrum, groups that see themselves as loosely bound communities of believers can be so egalitarian that there is an inbuilt resistance to anyone using gifts related to leadership or authority, even the appropriate kind that is based on God's Word. But even the great number of true churches that fill the middle ground between the two poles can have long-held assumptions and traditions that stifle the potential growth of individuals. Groups that are being impacted in continually fresh ways by the Truth review this regularly and honestly, making adjustments to ensure they are creating opportunities for non-specialist, less established, newer and younger disciples to demonstrate their God-given gifts and abilities to serve the Church locally and further afield.

It's also worth noting that there can be *cultural* obstacles. Back in Tutorial 7.13 we considered some cultural spectrums that relate to *Identity*. Those that focus on contrasting views of authority and status are also very relevant to this area of Discipleship we're addressing here. For example, a church that exists in a *High Power Distance* community (where inequalities in authority and status are accepted as inevitable, power is held close and distinctions are accentuated) can unthinkingly perpetuate a wide gulf between those with authority and those who have none. Similarly, a church in what's termed an *Ascribed Status* culture (that views prestige as inherent in the person and difficult to lose, where power is automatic and related to social class or affiliations, and where titles are important) will have to consciously work against those cultural defaults. The evidence of God's Word is all against the idea of the Spirit giving gifts to God's people based on status or family connections. There's certainly good reasons to respect the wisdom that can come with age, and there's nothing inherently wrong with titles, but discipleship is suffocated when older members and those in positions of authority aren't actively encouraging the next generation and giving opportunities for ministry to all other qualified members of the fellowship.

Paternalism vs. Discipleship

One way of describing the conditions that either inhibit or promote an atmosphere in which all of God's children are able to grow in their gifts and fulfil their God-given potential is to contrast *paternalism* with *discipleship*. (Note that paternalism is most often a description used in cross-cultural work, but it is equally apt in other situations as well. Also note that it's not only men who can have the attitudes we're describing here under either of these terms.)

Paternalism	Discipleship
assumes superiority	wants to bring about equality
parent - child relationship	sibling - sibling relationship
perpetuates status quo	has a goal and purpose
protects knowledge and position	freely shares insights and roles
defines a vision for others	draws others to God's purpose and vision
thinks in the immediate	has a view to the big picture
judges arbitrarily	defines relevant principles
responds to failure with disapproval	sees failures as an opportunity for equipping
referee	playing coach

Paternalism is the assumption of innate superiority – which might be based on education, social status, material possessions, technological know-how or sometimes even the assumption of spiritual superiority. *Paternalism* always condescendingly comes from above. In its most foundational sense, it describes a person taking the position of father or mother and relating to those around them as children who will always need guidance, protection and discipline. *Paternalism* serves to perpetuate the status quo, and has a stifling effect on the growth of younger or newer believers because they are not trusted and aren't placed in positions of responsibility, where they would have opportunities to grow by trusting the Lord. *Paternalism* is often short-sighted and only views people in terms of the shortcomings and lacks that exist now, rather than the potential for the future. Often people are only accepted or valued on the basis of their performance, and failure is met with disapproval rather than being seen as an opportunity for growth.

Discipleship, by contrast, is based on our relationship with the Lord and our understanding of how He relates to us. The true discipler wants to see this believer, student or co-worker grow to his or her own level of maturity and beyond. They are not content for the relationship to be a static one, because they expect others to become mature as they interact with God and His Word. Unlike paternalism – which passes judgment arbitrarily on each situation as it arises – discipleship looks for the underlying principle to pass on so that the other person is then equipped to deal with similar issues in the future. The paternalist acts like a referee – someone whose only involvement in the game is to see the rules are enforced, whereas the discipler sees him or herself in the temporary position of playing coach. *Discipleship* works *alongside* another person – it empathises and associates with the one being discipled – it looks forward to the time when this person is better equipped to play their part within God's purposes. For the true discipler, his or her own status doesn't enter into the picture because they are intent on doing all they can to help bring the other person to a level of maturity in Christ.

Some extra questions

To go along with the fourth question in the area of *Discipleship*, 'Are they being encouraged to function in the areas in which God has gifted and given them abilities so they can develop in their service to Him and His Body?' we can also ask:

- Are they being discipled into areas of service or are they being held back by personal, systemic or cultural barriers?
- Are opportunities being created for the expression of spiritual gifts and is there scope for people to explore appropriate ways to use their experience and skills?
- Is there a paternalism that stifles the growth of younger, newer and less mature believers OR is there a vision for discipleship that actively works to bring them to places of equality and hands authority over in a timely way?

The fifth question under "D" for *Discipleship*

- Are they seeing all other ties, loyalties and commitments being increasingly defined by their primary relationship: disciples of their Master, Jesus Christ?
- Are they being helped to apply the general truth from God's Word to their own specific real-life situations?
- Are they able to access regular, godly input and genuine friendships that intentionally help them along as they follow Jesus in the walk of faith?
- Are they being encouraged to function in the areas in which God has gifted and given them abilities so they can develop in their service to Him and His Body?
- <u>Do they have access to defined pathways that offer Bible-based resources, practical instruction and relational discipleship to adequately equip them to serve the church locally and globally?</u>

Facilitating discipleship

Up to this point, it has been mainly the natural colours and shades of relationships and the "organic" connections with Christ and His Body that have made up the portrait of discipleship that has emerged. But now, as we discuss this fifth and final question, it's important to recognise that defining some firmer outlines on the picture doesn't have to detract from the beauty that God has built into it. The key here is being sure that any structures or programs do actually facilitate the relationships that help Jesus' disciples to grow and be better equipped, and avoid the trap of becoming ends in themselves. The need to do this - to avoid this trap - provides a compelling argument for the local church being heavily engaged in preparing its members for roles of service, whether as part of the Body in its local community or as an extension into other communities.

It's not our purpose here to debate the relative benefits of Christian tertiary education or academic theological studies - obviously there are cultural contexts and denominational traditions that value them highly and see them as indispensable. Strong arguments are put forward for the benefits of maintaining a rigorous standard in theology and Christian education. A case is also made for certain specialist training (e.g. for cross-cultural workers, missionaries etc.) to take place on campuses where students rub shoulders with others headed to similar ministries and with experienced field practitioners. Whatever the potential benefits, these educational and training programs do run the risk of taking on a life of their own, a life that exists outside of the discipleship and oversight of the local church. Churches that are committed to discipleship principles may use these facilities for some components of equipping their members, but they don't abdicate responsibility for their care to professional educators, experts in a particular field or so-called *para-church* organisations. Godly parents, mature believers and leaders within the church who've developed relationships of trust with younger believers, for example, continue to maintain those friendships, helping them process new information and experiences - they don't abdicate responsibility, assuming that everything their people are exposed to in Christian establishments will help them to follow Jesus or even to serve Him more effectively.

We're not trying to paint a picture of believers having every aspect of their lives micro-managed by their home fellowships, dictating choices about where they can or can't go to pursue avenues of work and ministry. But younger, newer believers need to know that they have access to good advice and counsel, and that others who've walked the road of discipleship ahead of them are keeping up to date on currents in the culture and trends within the wider Church. As they move forward in their careers and prepare to contribute to God's purposes, it is vital for them to be able to process decisions with other believers they like and respect, and whom they can trust to give positive, honest input.

Fellowships that are serious about playing a role in discipling their people in a wider sense, do their homework; based on their understanding from His Narrative, they articulate His perspectives and how He is working in the world; they define priorities for the kinds of efforts they will give the bulk of their resources to; they can speak intelligently to their people about different avenues, teams, and organisations they believe are committed to the same priorities and values; they work to understand the different challenges involved; they have thoughts too on what gifts and abilities are best suited to different roles; they have a level of understanding about what kinds of equipping are appropriate for those roles; they determine whether they, as a church, have the necessary resources to see their people equipped for roles God is leading them together into; and they seek out what they are lacking or "out-source" where they lack.

All too often a dichotomy is perpetuated between full-time, "professional" or "supported" Christian ministries (e.g. pastors, missionaries, Christian counsellors) and other ways that people serve Jesus as His disciples (e.g. elders and deacons, "lay" teachers in the church, administrators, worship leaders, church Sunday school teachers, small group facilitators, witnesses in daily life). One problem with categorising roles in these different ways is the frequent assumption that yes, of course, those in the first group need training, while everyone else will just somehow learn to be effective through experience. Churches with a broader perspective of discipleship don't make these assumptions; always against the backdrop of relational discipleship, they offer access to practical and, where appropriate, "technical" help to prepare their people beforehand as well as "on the job".

Hopefully, through these resources we've made a compelling case for God's Narrative itself being the primary equipping tool for disciples of Jesus, no matter what path He leads them on in their lives and service for Him. Any other additional training program or curriculum should be firmly tied in to that overarching perspective provided by God's Word - a *Biblical theology* - and be a practical outworking of the principles and values it reveals.

Some extra questions

To go along with the fifth question in the area of *Discipleship*, 'Do they have access to defined pathways that offer Bible-based resources, practical instruction and relational discipleship to adequately equip them to serve the church locally and globally?' we can also ask:

- Is there a sense of responsibility taken in the church to be informed about current trends, needs and opportunities so that members can be given valid input as they move towards new opportunities for service?

- Are the ministry values, priorities and objectives of the church shared regularly with the whole Body, in smaller contexts, and in discipleship relationships?
- Does the church have a vital interest and sense of responsibility in seeing all members properly equipped to be effective disciple-makers, OR do they draw a false dichotomy between "full-time, professional, specialists ministries" and other "normal walks of life"?

....

Stefan's Story

When Stefan decided to ride his bike to the university a different way than normal one morning, he was surprised to see a line of buses outside the old abandoned football stadium that was usually the haunt of graffiti artists and drug dealers. Later he saw on a news site that the Munich city authorities had run out of apartments for all the Syrian refugees flooding in and were now housing them in zeltlager - tent camps - wherever they could find some empty space. As a kid he'd heard his grandparents talk about their escape from a grim, tyrannical Czech Republic back in the sixties, and how, although they were grateful to be granted asylum, what a struggle it was to build a new life here in West Germany, especially because not everyone welcomed them with open arms. His heart went out now to these latest refugees who'd lost everything in a nightmare war they had no part in starting. Coming from just east of the border, at least his grandparents had spoken some German when they arrived, but these Syrians faced the huge barrier of learning a completely new language. Talking to God, he wondered how he might be able to help and show them Jesus' love.

Two days later he met up for coffee with Max, a leader of the student Bible study group Stefan had joined when he moved to Munich a year ago to study graphic design. Max was probably in his late thirties or even forties, but he didn't really seem that old. It always surprised him a bit when he remembered that Max was part of the church pastoral staff, because he seemed like just a good friend now. Okay, he liked electronic music from the 80s and often wore checked shirts, but apart from that he was pretty cool. The small fourth floor apartment he shared with his wife Daniela and their dog Luther had become a home away from home for Stefan and some other students here in the big city.

Now, sitting in their favorite armchairs at the coffee shop where they always met up on Tuesday mornings, he casually mentioned to Max that he'd been thinking about maybe helping the Syrian refugees somehow. Max sat forward with an excited look on his face.

"It's amazing you bring that up," he said, "because the leadership team at church have been really burdened for those people. In fact, just the other day at our meeting we put that on our top five priorities for church projects. We did a bit of research and found a team that teaches Deutsch als Zweitsprache (German as a Second Language) to refugees. We think they might be believers, and wondered if we can partner somehow. We started praying about who from our fellowship might have an interest. I actually mentioned you as a possibility, but didn't know what you'd think."

Mapping out a plan became an excuse to order pastries. Stefan would find out more about the DZ team and report back. Max would let the leaders at church know and put out feelers for anyone else who'd be interested.

As it turned out, things moved quickly. Here he was already, Stefan thought, as he walked towards the community center to meet his first Syrian family, only five weeks after mentioning the idea to Max. It had been an intense month of fast tracking for DZ certification in what is normally a six-week course, and juggling that with normal studies. There had been a meeting with the refugee assistance organization he'd be working with, which turned out to be quite loosely structured and only nominally "Christian".

He'd gotten together with the church leadership team three different times. They'd been very supportive, and to his surprise, had treated him...well, just like one of them really, even though they were older guys like Max. In amongst the encouragement and jokes about his feeble attempt to grow a "contextual" beard, there were some probing questions about how he would approach this new challenge. It turned out that the leaders had been doing their own studies, months before the whole refugee thing had occurred to him, and were surprisingly well informed about different nuances of Islam; some had even made the effort to download the syllabus of the DZ course he'd done and knew enough to talk about methods of teaching German. They'd really liked some thoughts he'd had about not forcing things with anyone, just focusing on building friendships and allowing God to move things in good directions in His timing. But they did want to know how he'd handle questions about Christianity if they came up, and they even did some role-play that was really helpful until it fell apart with laughter as Max overdid the aggressive devil's advocate role.

Last Sunday morning, Andreas, one of the pastors, had interviewed him in front of the whole fellowship and asked a few people to come up and pray for him. That night, immersed in an assignment on manipulating digital images, he got a call from Max to say that after the service three other people from church had asked about also doing something to help the refugees. But the biggest surprise was that the leadership team wanted him, Stefan, to consider heading up a "Refugee response" team and to work closely with them in the process. He wondered if he was really up for the responsibility, but Max felt he was and said that he'd be glad to be an honorary member of the team and get together with them all for as long as Stefan wanted him to.

"Okay, here goes," he thought, as he opened the door and walked into the brightly lit gemeindezentrum (community center) where a stocky man with a beard, a lady with a headscarf and two kids were looking expectantly towards him.

❓ DISCUSSION POINTS

1. As you think back over your own path of discipleship so far please share anything you care to about any strengths or weaknesses you have noticed.

2. Imagine being involved in cross-cultural church planting in a previously unevangelised area: describe your "dream team" of partners and explain why you would choose to work with those people and that particular configuration.

3. Identify 6-10 features of relational discipleship in Stefan's story with a brief explanation.

4. Please share anything you care to that has particularly stood out, that you've learned, that has impacted you, or perhaps that you have questions about in this picture of discipleship presented in Tutorials 7.19-7.22.

Training Resources for Making Truth *Accessible*.

RESOURCES FOR

> Discipleship > Evangelism > Church Planting
> Language Learning > Bible Translation > Cross-cultural work

Equipping God's people to be more effective as they serve in cross-cultural contexts, either locally or globally.

accesstruth.com

www.ingramcontent.com/pod-product-compliance
Lightning Source LLC
Chambersburg PA
CBHW061928290426
44113CB00024B/2843